THE ARCHITECTURE OF FRANK LLOYD WRIGHT

The MIT Press
Cambridge, Massachusetts,
and London, England

THE ARCHITECTURE OF FRANK LLOYD WRIGHT

A Complete Catalog

Second Edition

William Allin Storrer

Twelfth printing, 1995

First MIT Press paperback edition, 1982

Original edition published in 1974 by The Massachusetts Institute of Technology, copyright © 1974 by William Allin Storrer.
Second edition published in 1978, new material copyright © 1978 by William Allin Storrer.

Printed and bound in the United States of America

Library of Congress Cataloging in Publication Data

Storrer, William Allin.
   The architecture of Frank Lloyd Wright.

   Includes indexes.
   1. Wright, Frank Lloyd, 1867-1959—Catalogs. I. Wright, Frank Lloyd, 1867-1959. II. Title.
NA737.W7A4 1978   720'.92'4   78-1306
ISBN 0-262-19171-7 (hard)
       0-262-69080-2 (paper)

To all those who,
like Frank Lloyd Wright,
recognize an organic way of life,
a beautiful life,
as the most desirable alternative
to ecological disaster.

FOREWORD

It is thirty years since *In The Nature of Materials,* the book that Frank Lloyd Wright had me prepare covering his work of the previous half century, appeared. A reprint is now available, but the coverage remains very incomplete. In the years since the last war, during which Mr. Wright continued in active production, the chronological limitation of *In The Nature of Materials* has become increasingly distressing to me and even more, surely, to the new generation of students, for they were at least as much interested in the then current work of the "Master" as in what he had produced in their grandparents' and their parents' time.

Publications by and about Frank Lloyd Wright have not ceased to appear. On the contrary, they have proliferated, so that the preparation of a complete bibliography of Wright and his work would be a very difficult, and even, since publication still continues, an unending, task. Grateful as we must be for the many existing reprints of early writings by and about Wright, not to speak of studies dealing more especially with his drawings and with his work in relation to that of his Middle Western contemporaries and followers, the present book is what has long been most needed. Here, for the first time, everything is included from the earliest houses for whose design the young Wright was responsible while in the employ of Sullivan to the semiposthumous buildings carried to completion by the Taliesin Associated Architects from Wright's extant designs since his death in 1959. With indefatigable assiduity Mr. Storrer has tracked down and photographed every structure there is good reason to believe was designed by Wright, even visiting the sites of demolished buildings. For the first time the entire Wrightian *oeuvre,* from his own house of 1889 in Oak Park, which still stands, though it has often been remodeled by him and others, to what survives across the Pacific in Japan. Graphic material, most particularly plans, could not be brought together to the same degree, as access to the Taliesin holdings has become, as is well known, all but impossible.

However thoroughly one may previously have known the work of Wright over the years—and I have had some familiarity with his work for forty years— there are innumerable surprises here, not merely as regards the work since the last war, never brought together before, but even for the early decades, the "classic" years of the Prairie house before World War I and the less productive years that immediately followed.

Mr. Storrer has performed an inestimable service not only in what he has amassed here but also in opening the way to a renewed study of the entire canon. I do not doubt that other young scholars will soon be following up clues that Mr. Storrer recurrently provides. His entries, in addition to giving present locations and describing the actual condition of extant buildings, include in many cases identification and analysis of later changes. Above all, the additional information he has brought together in several crucial instances will certainly affect understanding of the sequence of Wright's development. On the basis of the factual information and photographic imagery made available here, new interpretations of the immense variety in the seventy years of Wright's architectural production should emerge. When, eventually, what is offered here can be collated with the surviving graphic material, of which so little has been accessible thus far except when shown in special exhibitions, knowledge of Wright's work will exceed that of any other American architect.

Now, characteristic whole interiors by Wright are entering the collections of museums as well as single pieces of furniture—the living room of the Little house from Deephaven, Minnesota, in the Metropolitan Museum in New York and the Kaufmann Office from Pittsburgh in the Victoria and Albert Museum in London. Mr. Storrer's compilation has the great advantage of directing attention not merely to the particular qualities such interiors illustrate but to Wright's buildings as total architectural entities, from the smallest Usonian houses—one example of which, the Pope-Leighey house, is now preserved on a new site in Virginia by the National Trust—to the belatedly completed large-scale governmental buildings for Marin County in California. Finally, though Mr. Storrer disclaims the intention of providing any concerted critical consideration of Wright's work, the extent of his firsthand knowledge, unrivaled by that of any other scholar of his or an older generation, lends the innumerable decisions he has had to make a special authority. No one writing about Wright henceforth can afford to ignore what may be called the connoisseurship that has gone hand in hand with the accumulation of factual data and visual documentation. Although at one time I doubtless knew more of Wright's work of the period before 1940 than anyone else, I have been recurrently struck by refinements of the dating of well-known works here and the many minor structures, hitherto ignored, that are here included.

This is not primarily a picture book, filled though it is with pictures. Yet it should stimulate other photographers working in various regions to renewed attempts to produce with the camera images that for most students have remained those of the old Fuhrmann photographs, which have been so frequently reproduced over the past sixty years. This book represents the conclusion of Mr. Storrer's ambitious project, but it should also provide scholars the incentive to restudy critical aspects of the total Wright story that have unfortunately acquired the dubious authority of accepted myths.

Henry-Russell Hitchcock

ACKNOWLEDGMENTS

The author gratefully acknowledges the assistance
of the following individuals:
Bruce Brooks Pfeiffer
  of the Frank Lloyd Wright Foundation
Henry-Russell Hitchcock
Ben Raeburn
Bradley Ray Storrer
Denis C. Schmiedeke
Pete Pantaleo and Tom Moore, darkroom assistants
Rick Grabish
Raku Endo
Lloyd Wright
Eric Wright
John H. Howe
Harvey Ferrero

INTRODUCTION

To have seen every work of Frank Lloyd Wright that stands
today is like having heard every work of Beethoven, not
just the masterpieces. It occasions new thoughts on the
opus of America's best-known architectural genius. Fallingwater is a completely unique architectural creation, opening new vistas to architects willing to reach for the horizon,
yet one would hardly call it typical of Wright's work. What
is typical? Is there some ideal work that could be drawn
from the masterpieces known to every architectural student
of our century—Fallingwater, the Robie house, the second
Jacobs house (the solar hemicycle), La Miniatura, Ward
Willits' residence, Hollyhock house, to name some of the
most popular? No one of these looks vaguely like any of
the others here named.

Wright's output was so varied over the years that to try to
define any underlying principle would be presumptuous.
Possibly the principle of "organic architecture" is a fair solution, but then many would have expected some "style"
to have emerged in Wright's designs. Though several styles
did emerge, they correspond to changes in the architect's
life-style as much as to any other factor.

Wright's earliest work is largely eclectic. Even so, given
real freedom of choice, he could still design a Winslow residence that was unlike any of its neighbors and distinctly
"modern." The Prairie School style appeared in Wright's
work when, in his own studio and as his own boss, the architect received enough commissions to gather a staff, many
of whom later became well-known Prairie School architects
on their own. Wright's move to Taliesin brought further
changes, coupled with commissions on the West Coast. The
start of the Taliesin Fellowship in the Depression (with
Wright's first student, William Wesley Peters, now continuing
the work of the Fellowship as vice-president of the Frank
Lloyd Wright Foundation) brought about the Usonian house
as part of Broadacre City. Many later works that Wright
called "Usonian," such as the Pappas residence, bear little
visual resemblance to the first of the Usonian houses, the

first Jacobs residence, so we cannot even rely on Wright for stylistic terminology.

Accordingly, even though stylistic terms are used in the text, it has been my practice to employ them only in obvious cases or where historical precedent so dictates. The reader may make his own decisions about "styles" as he chooses.

I have tried to avoid drawing too many conclusions in this text, though I certainly have developed strong ideas while traveling 78,000 miles in search of every extant architectural work of Wright. It is the facts derived from my search that I wish to present, those facts about the structures themselves that seem incontestable. What constitutes a Wright building, and what does not? I have visited every building listed in this text that is not marked "demolished," and even for those buildings I have visited the sites. Photographs were made, though not without some difficulty. Several houses are so surrounded as to prevent a good foliage-free view. Although I should have liked to photograph each structure as Wright envisioned it in his presentation drawing, this too was largely impossible, if only due to a decade's tree growth since the last of Wright's projects was designed.

The basic starting point of my search was published lists of Wright's work—Bruce Radde's list in *Frank Lloyd Wright; Writings and Buildings,* edited by Ben Raeburn and Edgar Kaufmann; Bruce Brooks Pfeiffer's list in Olgivanna Lloyd Wright's *Frank Lloyd Wright, His Life, His Work, His Words;* as well as Henry-Russell Hitchcock's *In The Nature of Materials,* Grant Carpenter Manson's *Frank Lloyd Wright to 1910: The First Golden Age,* and hearsay from Wright homeowners, friends, and scholars. Buildings long since thought destroyed appeared (two buildings of the Como Orchard project), and many listed as built were simply not there. The Frank Lloyd Wright Foundation also has its own list of projects, which is based on plans in their archives, and and I have used this as a further guide. Where disagreement between my list and the Foundation's appeared, my own personal knowledge of the structure from my visit plus discussion with various architects and Wright scholars resolved the conflict to my satisfaction. (One example is the W. Irving Clark house in La Grange, Illinois. Hitchcock attributes this house to Wright's draftsman, Turnock, on the authority of Wright's own words.)

The important point I am making here is that no study of Wright can do the architect full justice if it ignores any of Wright's work. Yet nowhere has Wright's architectural opus been published *in toto.* Surely, we do discuss Attic Greek tragedy "with authority," though we possess not even forty complete works of the thousands that may have been written. To discuss Beethoven and Shakespeare, it is not necessary to know all their work, but it is helpful and may avoid costly error. The works of Wright that have been published over and over do constitute a fair cross section of his opus, particularly of the early years, but the later work is poorly represented in print.

This book documents all of Wright's architectural work. In an attempt to eliminate confusion about the "names" of Wright's buildings, the simplest possible system of personal identification is used. In almost all residences, the client's name suffices. In some instances only a line drawing and the name of the city or town where the house is located identifies the building. The names of the owners and the street addresses do not appear because we were unable to persuade the owners to join with us in producing this first complete catalog of Wright's work. For most nonresidential structures, the type of building is included as part of the identification. The boldfaced part of each entry in this volume is that part of the total name of each work that is needed for unique identification of the building. Although there is no standard term for residential works, if Wright's drawings can be taken as evidence of his own choice of terms, *residence* is preferred to any other identification; and this term has been used in the titles for the text listings, with other terminology employed in the body of the text for variety.

The book also identifies each extant project (though not every building within a project) by a photo or, in cases where foliage or the client's desire for privacy interfere, by a drawing. The photographs tend to show full views of each of the houses. Often achieved only by the use of ultrawide-angle lenses to overcome limitations of surrounding foliage, these photographs are as consistent as seems practical with Wright's own expression of the buildings as rendered in his presentation drawings. Wright carefully designed privacy into his residences, and the photograph or drawing here presented keeps this intent in mind, even when a less than satisfactory view is the result. Where suitable photographs or drawings of demolished buildings were made available to me, they are included with the text. The catalog lists the earliest known date for Wright's concept of the project, client, type of building, and, where it seems appropriate, such matter as the materials used in construction, some background on the client, the nature of the site, and super-vision of the project. (Where a more consistent picture of the chronological development of Wright's designs may be obtained, the construction date, representing all changes in the original design, is given instead of the concept date.) Beyond this outline, no standard format is followed in the text, any more than Wright had a specific formula for designing a house.

The question of supervision of projects is worthy of a whole book unto itself and is therefore given little space in this volume. It does raise a further question, that of authen-ticity of structures. Wright disowned structures built from his plans but slightly modified in construction—for exam-ple the boards of the second level of the George Spencer residence were laid vertically, although Wright "always" specified horizontal siding; however, such works are listed as by Wright in this study. Supervision was largely of three types—by Wright himself, by a builder whom Wright trusted implicitly from earlier work, or by a Taliesin Fellow. From the Depression on, Wright had one of the students of the Taliesin Fellowship live on the site of each project through-out the duration of construction. Occasionally the work of this Fellow bears comment for his later individual accom-plishments or his significance to the Frank Lloyd Wright

Foundation. Any project supervised by Wright, builder, or Taliesin Fellow is considered authentic. Any project built from Wright's plans but not supervised in one of these three ways, yet listed in the text, is so noted.

Projects are numbered in their order of appearance in their basic listing in the catalog. This order is largely chronological, but, as there is insufficient information to determine the exact order in which Wright conceived his project or obtained the commissions, no attempt has been made to give the works more than general chronological listing or numbering. Boldfaced numbers have been assigned to all buildings for which a photograph or drawing appears, while lightfaced numbers indicate that there is no illustration of this project.

The question of how many numbers should be applied to a project might be raised. A group of apartments built at one time as a contiguous group on a level site—Munkwitz or Richards are examples—is given a single project number. Three originally identical cottages—Mrs. Gale and Duplicate I and II—are individually numbered, since Wright located each on its site to take advantage of the lakeshore and sun position with respect to surrounding foliage.

The one possible deviation from this system might be in the numbering of additions to projects. Only those additions of Wright's design, of course, are considered. Where such additions to a project are for a client other than the original one, they are numbered under that client's name. Additions for the original client are usually not given a separate number; generally, the altered project in these few instances—McCartney is a fine example with its three closely spaced additions—remains so organically organized as to defy separation of the parts by even a well-trained eye. Such additions are noted by a letter suffix to the project number. Additions by the architect himself to his own residential "complexes"—his first home/studio, Taliesin, and Taliesin West—are separately numbered where they are sufficiently distinct units or where they mark steps in the continuous construction of the project.

Though a builder could have "pirated" a Wright plan, this

text lists no such works. In Wright's work, the design considered site shape and placement; site and house are one. Even today, when the Frank Lloyd Wright Foundation releases a Wright design to a new client, such release depends upon approval of a site suitable to Wright's original concept. A house not placed on the site in accordance with organic architectural principles would likely deny the creator's intention and therefore cannot qualify as authentically Wright. For this reason, pirated designs are not herein listed.

Nor are any of Wright's designs being built in the seventies listed. This category poses a problem to any specialist; these are Wright's by design, but how true to his conception is the current realization? If built on the same site as Wright intended and without other alteration, there would be little doubt as to authenticity. The designs are, however, available for different sites, and they are altered for modern appliances. Early Wright structures have been modernized, particularly in the kitchens and for the addition of air conditioning, and still command listing as Wright's work. Since none of these structures is complete at this writing, none is yet listed, though some may qualify as entries to the listing at a later date if Wright's concept of interior space remains unaltered. The 1959-designed Lykes house, though altered by John Rattenbury (in a manner I feel Wright would have approved of), for late-1960's construction, is the latest work listed.

Neither does this catalog include Wright's minor contributions to the work of other architects in whose offices he was employed. Manson mentions some possibilities, mostly connected with Wright's work in Silsbee's office, and there are some details in works of the office of Adler & Sullivan as well. These works belong properly to the office; only where Wright was entrusted with the entire project—the Charnley and Sullivan summer residences, for example—is it considered suitable for listing in this text.

Much information is left to the indexes, maps, and plans. Here the location information is more specific than in the text, giving geographical insights that may not be otherwise apparent, allowing quick checks on clients or building types (all buildings being listed according to Wright's/clients' intended use), and freeing the catalog to be organized in chronological fashion so that the photographs provide the reader with the greatest amount of comparative information.

The book cannot possibly exhaust the approaches to Wright's work or supply all the information everyone would like to find in it. It does, for the first time in history, list every Wright work that was built and identify in photo or drawing the extant constructed projects. It should give everyone interested in Wright's work—architect, student, or amateur enthusiast—the basis for expanding his knowledge of the infinite variety of architectural themes that constitutes three-quarters of a century's designing. Even the most careful scholar may find an aspect of Wright's work not before known to him.

William Allin Storrer

PREFACE TO THE SECOND EDITION

This second edition of *The Architecture of Frank Lloyd Wright* was occasioned by the many people who found in the first edition something they failed to find in other writings on Wright. Their interest overflowed into contributions of both facts and photographs. While benefiting from these offerings, this book remains what it was originally intended to be, a place to which one can turn for basic information about any, and every, work of Wrights's built oeuvre.

Both textual and photographic documentation have been expanded for this edition, and many matters of detail refined. Some structures have been removed from the catalog as spurious, only one added; in these instances of change, the hand of Walter Burley Griffin is often evident. Both indexes should be more useful than before: the geographical index because of added guides on the use of the zip code system by which it is organized, the alphabetical index because of added entries, particularly a cross-referencing of cities in which buildings were, or are, located. Drawings now appear only where there is hope that, one day, we may yet be able to insert a photograph.

This edition continues the comprehensive listing of Wright's constructed architectural work, with visual documentation of most buildings, and the compendium of facts on individual structures and Wright's career as an architectural designer. To be useful as a handy, if not quite pocket-sized, guide to Wright's work, it avoids encyclopedic detail. One seeking plans should look to studies of a different nature than this. Bibliographical material is best found in such listings as J. R. Muggenberg's 1972 updating of Bernard Karpel's seminal compilation.

Interest in Wright is waxing strong. His distinctive solutions to energy and space problems command respect thirty or more years late, but maybe not too late. There are still areas of Wright's work insufficiently studied; none are here intentionally slighted. May this book, then, continue to serve as a place where neophyte and sophisticate alike may turn, one to begin a rewarding exploration of the many dimensions of the architectural genius of Frank Lloyd Wright, the other to find new areas worthy of fuller exploration concerning the architect's ever-new insights into meeting human needs.

William Allin Storrer

THE ARCHITECTURE OF FRANK LLOYD WRIGHT

CATALOG OF FRANK LLOYD WRIGHT BUILDINGS

1 Nell and Jane Lloyd Jones, **Hillside Home School I** (1887)
Spring Green, Wisconsin
Demolished, 1950

Wright's aunts, Nell and Jane Lloyd Jones, taught in this
private school for many years. Eventually, a larger, more
complex structure was erected in 1903 (69).

2, 3 **Frank Lloyd Wright Residence** (1889), **Playroom Addition**
4 (1893), and **Studio** (1895)
Oak Park, Illinois

The oldest extant house by Wright is surfaced with wood
shingles. In the interior space the architect defines door
tops with string courses rather than the more common
architraves. Adjacent to the house is the shingles-and-brick
studio, erected in 1898. Because Wright was his own client,
his expression was not reserved; ornament became one with
architecture, structure and design one with each other, and
the whole and its parts could not be separated. The octagon, one of Wright's favorite geometrical forms during the
earlier years, appears in the plan of the library. Eventually
Wright moved to Taliesin. These structures were remodeled
into apartments by Wright in 1911. Further remodeling,
and some restoration, was undertaken by Clyde Nooker
(405) in 1956. The Frank Lloyd Wright Residence has been
designated by the American Institute of Architects (AIA) as
one of seventeen American buildings designed by this architect to be retained as an example of his architectural contribution to American culture. The Frank Lloyd Wright Home
and Studio Foundation is in charge of preservation of these
buildings and conducts tours of the premises.

Playroom Addition and Studio

5, 6 Louis Sullivan Summer Residence and **Stables** (1890)
Ocean Springs, Mississippi
Stables demolished, 1942

Located directly on the Gulf Coast, this house was part of a
group of Wright-designed buildings on adjacent lots (5-8).
Its high-pitched roof is characteristic, not of Louis Sullivan,
but of the young Wright to whom the "Lieber Meister" had
delegated the work. In 1970 a new dining room was added
to the east half of the south facade, permanently altering
Wright's T plan. There are many other alterations, mostly
from restoration in the 1930s, but the woodwork in several
rooms remains in fine condition.

7, 8 James **Charnley Summer Residence** and **Guesthouse** (1890)
Ocean Springs, Mississippi

The main structure is a very large version of the neighboring
Sullivan house (5) and was preferred by Wright to the
"Lieber Meister's" residence. Its T plan features bay windows of octagonal geometry, and the guesthouse (at the left
in the photograph) originally was a large octagon divided
by a single wall into two rooms. The building was restored
in the 1930s and later altered. The northeast porch has
been considerably enlarged, both side porches enclosed,
and the wood front steps replaced with brick. Otherwise,
this structure is in remarkably good condition.

9 James **Charnley Residence** (1891)
Chicago, Illinois

While Sullivan was busy with larger commercial works, Wright gained the opportunity to do some of the office's domestic commissions, including the Charnley house. It was a statement far beyond its time in terms of the simplicity of the ornamentation and in the way the exterior reflected interior space. Although the house was originally symmetrical about an east-west axis, a later addition (cropped from the photograph) squared off the dining room bay window on the south facade.

10 W. S. **MacHarg** Residence (1891)
Chicago, Illinois
Demolished

Even while gaining some of Sullivan's domestic commissions, Wright was working at night on commissions of his own, unknown to the firm of Adler & Sullivan and against the express provisions of his five-year contract with them. The MacHarg (or possibly, McHarg) house is the first of nine of these that were constructed in this manner.

11, 12 Warren **McArthur Residence** (1892), **Residence Remodeling**
13 (1900), and **Stable** (1900)
Chicago, Illinois

In the McArthur residence, another of Wright's moonlighted
projects, Roman brick is used up to the window sill, and
plaster above. The stable has been remodeled since Wright's
work. To the immediate south is the Blossom residence (14)
and garage (133). The McArthur family was an important
Wright client. E. E. Boynton (147) learned of Wright
through McArthur. In the mid-twenties Wright's collaboration with McArthur's son Albert on the Arizona Biltmore
Hotel (221, 222) may have been the initial step to the even-
tual establishment of Taliesin West as winter home for the
Fellowship.

14 George **Blossom Residence** (1892)
Chicago, Illinois

With this house, Wright demonstrated that, had he so chosen, he could have been one of the greatest of academic architects. The work is a fine example of academic Colonial Revival. With the exception of the rear extension to the conservatory, visible in rear view photograph, the plan is symmetrical. The house is of clapboard siding, and the dormers are a later addition. This is another of the moonlighted, or "bootlegged" (to use Grant Manson's term), houses.

15 Robert G. **Emmond** Residence (1892)
LaGrange, Illinois

Another moonlighting venture while Wright was with Adler
& Sullivan, the Emmond house is the most elaborate of
three houses using the same T plan, in each case set sideways to the street. The Emmond, though, is symmetrical
about a north-south axis, while the Thomas H. Gale and
Parker (located only three lots apart in Oak Park) are
turned onto east-west axes. All three were originally clapboard structures, but the Emmond has been resurfaced with
brick on its lower story; the terraces have also been enclosed,
and the house otherwise considerably altered. The Emmond
dwelling is across the street from the Goan residence (29).

16 Thomas H. Gale Residence (1892)
Oak Park, Illinois

Though a copy in plan of the Emmond (15) and Parker (17) houses, the Thomas H. Gale residence apparently pleased Mrs. Gale. She had two designs by Wright built in the first decade of the 1900s, a cottage (88) and a home (98).

17 R. P. **Parker** Residence (1892)
Oak Park, Illinois

Before the porch was destroyed, the Parker house was iden-
tical in plan to the Emmond and Thomas H. Gale residences.
In the photographic background to the Parker house is the
Walter Gale dwelling (20).

18 Allison **Harlan** Residence (1892)
Chicago, Illinois
Demolished, 1963

Of the many houses Wright moonlighted while with the firm of Adler & Sullivan, this stands out both in design and as the one that probably caused Wright's separation from the firm. The facade is not broken by an entryway; rather, that is placed on the side facing south (left in the photograph), as in the McArthur (11) and later Heller (38) residences, and is reached via a walled walkway. The living room, though it was later altered at Dr. Harlan's insistence, originally spanned the full width of the facade. Full-width terrace and second-story balcony further emphasize the horizontal aspect of the structure. The demolition of this and two other South Side Chicago works designed by Wright came about under curious circumstances. All three were designed in the early 1890s. The Harlan house was demolished first, then the Albert Sullivan dwelling (19), and the Francis Apartments (32) last. Each was destroyed without any adjacent buildings being damaged. In the early seventies, both the Harlan and Albert Sullivan lots were still vacant while the original neighbors remained. A year after the demolition of the Francis Apartments, the lot remains vacant, while old neighbors remain.

19 Albert Sullivan Residence (1892)
Chicago, Illinois
Demolished, 1970

The facade of this row-house design of two floors and basement reveals Sullivanian tracery in its detail. Louis Sullivan, Wright's "Lieber Meister," lived here some four years before his brother occupied the quarters. This and other Louis Sullivan (5, 6) and James Charnley (7, 8, 9) buildings could all be attributed to the "Lieber Meister" on the principle that all originated from his office, and Wright designed in Sullivan's manner, not as he would have had the commissions been his own.

20 Walter M. Gale Residence (1893)
Oak Park, Illinois

Although Sullivan gave Wright several projects in Ocean Springs (5-8) and the Charnley project in Chicago (9), Wright moonlighted other works of this period. Most reveal but little of the Wright work that was to come in the year this house was designed. The clapboard Walter M. Gale house has lost its front terrace but otherwise appears much as constructed. It is located immediately west of the Parker house (17).

21 Robert M. **Lamp Cottage**, Rocky Roost (1893)
Governor's Island, Lake Mendota, Wisconsin
Demolished

Though living in Oak Park at this time, Wright maintained
contact with his native area around Madison, Wisconsin.
Two works came from this association in 1893, both on the
shores of the lake that often inspired him to his best
achievements. One of these was for "Robie" Lamp, a boy-
hood friend who was also to have a Wright-designed home
eleven years later (97). It cannot be determined with any
assurance how closely Rocky Roost adhered to Wright's
plan. The photograph was taken at about the time the
Lamp residence was in construction. (Photograph courtesy
of the Iconographic Collection, State Historical Society of
Wisconsin.)

22 Madison Improvement Association, **Municipal Boathouse** (1893)
Madison, Wisconsin
Demolished, 1928

In May of this year Wright won a competition for design of the Municipal Boathouse. Its large arch, facing the lake (at the left of the photograph), may also be seen as a design feature of later lakeside structures, such as the Jones house (83) and the George Gerts Double House (77).

23 Francis **Wooley** Residence (1893)
Oak Park, Illinois

South of the Thomas H. Gale house (16) is the Wooley residence. Probably originally built of clapboards, it has been resurfaced with an imitation brick siding.

24, 25 William H. **Winslow Residence** and **Stable** (1893)
River Forest, Illinois

The Winslow residence, designed for the publisher of *House Beautiful*, was Wright's first independent commission after he left the offices of Adler & Sullivan. Already one may note stylistic characteristics that were to stay with Wright throughout his life; a stylobate-like foundation that firmly sets the house on the earth, living quarters that dominate the structure, broad overhanging eaves, and, in two-story structures, a second story that is like a gallery, never dominating the first floor. In the Winslow house, the masonry elements are treated to a foliage ornament in the manner of Louis Sullivan. Tapestry brick of Roman dimensions is the basic material, while stone and plaster are also employed. Here, double-hung windows are used, a rarity among the architect's "modern" designs: casement windows were the norm. The porte-cochere on the north was balanced in Wright's plan by an intended-but-not-built pavilion on the south, of the architect's ubiquitous (in early years) octagonal geometry. The southeast corner porch (not visible in the photograph) was enlarged and enclosed by architect Norman Steenhof in 1962. A plan of the main floor, as originally constructed, may be found following this catalog section. This structure has been designated by the American Institute of Architects as one of seventeen American buildings designed by Wright to be retained as an example of his architectural contribution to American culture.

Winslow Stable

26 Robert W. **Roloson Apartments** (1894)
Chicago, Illinois

The first of Wright's "apartment" projects, this complex is actually his only executed example of city row houses. The stone work is abstract, not Gothic. The northernmost unit has been painted over its brown brick. Roloson was a son-in-law of Edward C. Waller (see 30, 31, 47, 65, 66).

27   H. W. **Bassett** Residence **Remodeling** (1894)
Oak Park, Illinois
Demolished

No records are available to indicate the nature of this remodeling for Dr. Bassett.

28   Frederick Bagley Residence (1894)
Hinsdale, Illinois

Many of Wright's early houses reflect the eclectic tastes of
the clients. The Frederick Bagley dwelling reveals the influence of J. L Silsbee on Wright and, perhaps, also of H. H.
Richardson. It is of stained wood shingles, now painted a
lighter color. The veranda is of stone, and the northern
structure, the library (at left in the photograph), is octagonal in plan.

29 Peter **Goan** Residence (1894)
LaGrange, Illinois

Wright never expressed any love of clapboard in his later
years; board and batten, laid horizontally, were his clear
preference in wood construction. Here we see them in the
Goan house, which, over the years, has lost a full-width
front terrace and second-story porch, which added to the
horizontal character of the structure in a manner similar to
the Harlan residence plan (18). Located directly across the
street from the Emmond house (15), it is also near the first
Hunt residence (138) and is the last of the designs Wright
moonlighted while with the firm of Adler & Sullivan.

30 Edward C. Waller, **Francisco Terrace Apartments** (1895)
Chicago, Illinois
Demolished, March 1974 (entry archway reconstructed at
Euclid Place, Oak Park, August 1977)

Edward C. Waller, neighbor of William H. Winslow (24, 25)
in Auvergne Place, was one of Wright's most important
early clients, and Waller's son commissioned the Midway
Gardens (180). In 1895 Waller built two sets of apartments
at the corner of Francisco and West Walnut streets. Francisco Terrace was the more original of the two, reaching deep
into its allotted space, with a half-circle archway forming
the entrance to the interior court. All but the street-front
apartments opened onto this courtyard, much like a mid-
twentieth-century motel. The second-story balcony was of
wood, and there were back porches, also of wood. General
neglect led to vandalism, then demolition. The archway has
been preserved on Lake Street at Euclid Place.

31 Edward C. **Waller Apartments** (1895)
Chicago, Illinois
Partially demolished

The Waller Apartments, five units planned for Jackson Boulevard and Kedzie Avenue, were not supervised in construction by Wright. Entry detail varies, but plans do not. The fifth unit from the east is shown in the photograph; the fourth has been demolished. The others, like Francisco Terrace around the corner, are threatened with the same fate already suffered by the Francis Apartments (32), demolition due to urban blight.

32 Terre Haute Trust Company, **Francis Apartments** (1895)
Chicago, Illinois
Demolished, 1971

The ground floor of this four-story structure was surfaced
with a geometrical pattern in the manner of Sullivan. Upper
floors had eight apartments of four to five rooms each. The
north wing on the ground floor contained four shops. This
photograph shows the Francis Apartments shortly before
demolition. (Photograph courtesy of Oak Park Public
Library.)

33 Chauncey L. **Williams** Residence (1895)
River Forest, Illinois

With its steeply pitched roof, articulation of plaster between eaves, and Roman brick below the sill line, this dwelling creates a colorful impression. It has undergone some interior remodeling. Wright made several designs for the dormers, at least two of which have been used at separate times.

34, 35 Nathan G. **Moore Residence** and **Stable** (1895)
Oak Park, Illinois

This Roman brick house, which is intentionally Tudor in character, was built in 1895, then rebuilt above the first floor in 1923 after a 1922 fire. Located directly north of the Hills residence (51), which Moore executed for his daughter, it is also across the street from the Heurtley house (74). The stable is at the far left in the photograph.

36 H. R. **Young** Residence **Alterations** (1895)
Oak Park, Illinois

Wright contributed only alterations, particularly at the main
level, to this structure. It is located only half a block from
the Mrs. Thomas H. Gale house (98).

37 Nell and Jane Lloyd Jones, **Romeo and Juliet Windmill** (1896)
Spring Green, Wisconsin

In Romeo and Juliet, the plan reveals a diamond interlocked with an octagon. This supposedly suggests Romeo
and Juliet, Shakespeare's lovers, clutching each other. Construction was in the fall of 1897, about a year after the idea
for the windmill was probably first conceived. The *Weekly
Home News* of Spring Green suggests 1897 as both the conception and construction date. In 1939 (right photograph)
the original wood shingles were replaced with horizontal
boards and battens.

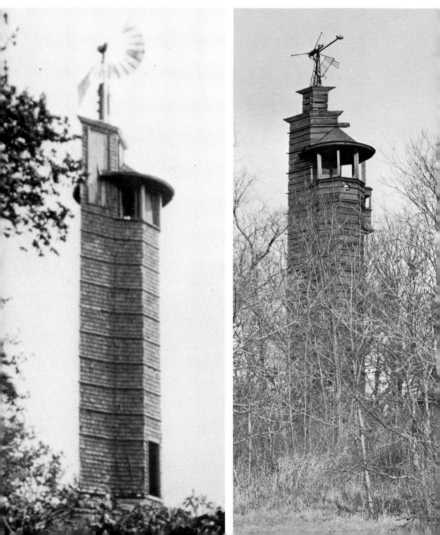

38 Isidore **Heller** Residence (1896)
Chicago, Illinois

The Heller house is essentially an I plan of rectangular interlocking spaces. The living room has a north-south orientation that crosses the long rectangle of the primary east-west
axis through the entry hallway to the dining room. This
dining room maintains the east-west orientation but is offset south of the prime axis. Space flows freely and draws
one from the entry to the larger living and dining quarters.
The exterior is of Roman brick, with the third story decorated in sculptured figures (not nude, as some texts suggested, but draped) by Richard Bock. The downspout in
the photograph is a later addition. The stable, shown on
plans and previously listed as item 39, was apparently not
built.

40 **Charles E. Roberts Residence Remodeling** and
41 **Stable Remodeling** (1896)
Oak Park, Illinois

Wright's work on the two Charles Roberts structures seems
to have been limited to remodeling. In the house, work was
confined to two main floor rooms and the stairwell and
perhaps a southwest upstairs library. String courses, not
architraves, define door tops, and the woodworking is well
preserved. At the time of the house remodeling the stable
was at the rear of the same lot. If Wright provided any alterations for it, they did not survive a 1929 remodeling for use
as a dwelling and relocation to an adjacent lot, by Charles
E. White, Jr. No plans or drawings by Wright for work on
the structure have been found.

42 Harry C. **Goodrich** Residence (1896)
Oak Park, Illinois

Though the plan may have come from one of four low-cost
designs originally offered to Charles Roberts (40) and may
date from 1895, the house was built in the summer of
1896. Many elements point to later Wright compositions.
The second-story windows are located directly below the
eaves and are linked horizontally by the light color of the
clapboards (which are original). The lower boards conceal a
basement that is partly above ground. The once-open porch
has been enclosed and the interior altered.

43 George Furbeck Residence (1897)
Oak Park, Illinois

The George Furbeck house no longer appears as originally constructed. The brown brick and wood trim remain, but the porch has been enlarged and enclosed, altering Wright's proportions.

44 Rollin Furbeck Residence (1897)
Oak Park, Illinois

The cruciform plan of the Rollin Furbeck house is slightly altered by the entry porch and by a porte-cochere, which has since been removed. The light tan brick and colored wood trim are part of a three-story facade articulated in both surface and color. The hipped roof is employed by the architect, and the upper-story windows hug the broad, overhanging eaves in a band of stucco. This, and the house for Rollin's brother George (43), was most likely a wedding gift from their father Warren Furbeck.

45 George W. Smith Residence (1896)
Oak Park, Illinois

This house, built in 1898, may come from a plan first submitted in 1896 to Charles Roberts (40) as part of a group of four low-cost homes for Ridgeland, Illinois. Its use of shingles looks back to earlier years; Wright would soon employ horizontal board and batten siding, a hallmark of many Prairie and Usonian structures.

46 Joseph **Husser** Residence (1899)
Chicago, Illinois
Demolished

The Husser dwelling takes several strides forward toward the soon-to-emerge Prairie house style. Wright apparently never liked "cellars." He eliminated them altogether in the Usonian house principles; in the Prairie house he raised living quarters above ground level. In the Husser residence, the basement was at ground level, and the house rose yet two floors higher, thereby affording a magnificent view of nearby Lake Michigan. This design innovation may also be seen as a means of avoiding flooding of living quarters. Octagonal elements appear in the plan, breaking the monotony of rectilinearity. A favored plan of Prairie style dwellings, the cruciform, appears in the west-east extensions of a basically north-south structure in the entryway stairwell and the dining room overlooking Lake Michigan. The surface ornamentation is reminiscent of Sullivan. A plan of the principal floor is at the rear of this book, following the catalog section.

47   Edward C. **Waller Residence Remodeling** (1899)
River Forest, Illinois
Demolished

Though Wright produced many designs for Edward C.
Waller, few—principally, only two apartment projects (30,
31)—came to fruition. This remodeling of a large house in
Auvergne Place across the street from William Winslow (24,
25) included the dining room and other interior work. In
1899 Wright kept a Chicago office in the Rookery Building
(113), managed by Waller. Winslow was another Rookery
tenant at that time.

48   **Jessie M. Adams** Residence (1900)
Chicago, Illinois

Plans and county records indicate that this house, long
attributed to a William Adams, was designed for Mrs. Jessie
M. Adams and date it to November 1900. The exterior is
hardly Wrightian, double-hung windows being particularly
out of place. Some suggest a foreshadowing of the "Fireproof House for $5,000" (138). (Photograph courtesy of
W. R. Hasbrouck, AIA.)

49, 50 S. A. **Foster Residence** and **Stable** (1900)
Chicago, Illinois

Though Wright had not yet visited Japan, the roof lines of this dwelling, curved and rising toward their extremities, suggest an Oriental influence. Perhaps the source is Wright's extensive knowledge of Japanese prints. Wright's first visit to Japan was in 1905.

51 Edward R. **Hills** Residence (1906)
Oak Park, Illinois

Heavily damaged by fire on January 3, 1976, reconstruction was begun immediately. The Hills house originally sat in what is now the backyard of the Nathan Moore dwelling (34). Though Wright remembered the project as dating to 1900, that is apparently six years too early. Moore had the house moved and remodeled in 1906 for his daughter Mary and her husband Edward. Broad overhangs and the banding of the stucco surface place this design in the context of 1906 Prairie styles.

52 B. Harley **Bradley Residence**, "Glenlloyd," and
53 **Stable** (1900)
Kankakee, Illinois

In Glenlloyd the influence of Japanese prints on Wright becomes quite apparent. Because of the porte-cochere, which extends the wing on the left in the photograph, the cruciform plan shows clearly in the exterior. Plaster with wood trim and leaded-glass windows articulate the surface. It was built for Mrs. Bradley, sister of Mrs. Charles Roberts (40, 41) and Warren Hickox (56). Located on the right bank of the Kankakee River, this large residential structure with stable has been converted into a restaurant, "Yesteryear," and gift shop. To the immediate north is the Hickox house (56), which may have been used as the builder's office/house while Glenlloyd was being constructed.

54 Ward W. **Willits Residence** (1901)
Highland Park, Illinois

The Ward Willits home represents a radical step forward in
Wright's emerging design maturity. Gone are the suggestions
of Tudor half-timber construction, such as remain in Glenlloyd (52). Here is the first house in true Prairie style, with
living quarters raised above ground level. One must pass
through a series of alternating expansive—porte-cochere,
stairwell—and compressive—entry, short stairway, and left
turn—spaces to reach the main living area (a plan may be
found following the catalog section in this book). Each
wing, in a pinwheel configuration visually blocked one from
the other by a massive central fireplace and woodwork, is
quite spacious. The living room relates the in-dweller to the
site in a manner new to Wright's work. Its end wall is floor-
to-ceiling glass, open to the yard, to nature, across a large
terrace. On the sides, high windows lead the eye neither to
neighbor's home nor ground but the sky. From this concept, the Prairie ideal would develop to more open, yet
interlocked, spaces. Structural steel is concealed within the
walls; wood and plaster therein give hint of later steel and
concrete designs. This structure has been designated by the
AIA as one of seventeen American buildings designed by
Frank Lloyd Wright to be retained as an example of his
architectural contribution to American culture.

55 Ward W. **Willits Gardener's Cottage with Stables** (1901)
Highland Park, Illinois

Behind the Willits Residence stands a gardener's cottage, shown in most of the renderings from Wright's office but rarely considered separately from the main house. This wood and plaster structure in the Prairie idiom, with attached stables, has been remodeled.

56 Warren **Hickox** Residence (1900)
Kankakee, Illinois

When the wood members of this type of house become less structurally obvious in the Tudor half-timber sense, as they do in the Henderson residence (57), the house becomes a Prairie style structure. The Hickox residence is located just north of its client's brother-in-law's residence, the Bradley house (52).

57 F. B. **Henderson** Residence (1901)
Elmhurst, Illinois

In terms of plan, the Henderson is a virtual mirror of the
Hickox structure (56), both T plans set sideways to the
main road. The Hickox, however, has a gabled roof and
octagonal bay windows, while the Henderson has a hipped
roof, making it more apparently a Prairie house. The house
was done in collaboration with Webster Tomlinson, the
only "partner" Wright ever had. In later years, a covered,
second-story porch was added, over the original terrace, at
the living room. Joan and Roger A. Schmiege restored the
house to its original design in 1975.

58 William G. **Fricke** (Fricke-Martin) **Residence** (1901) and
59, **60** **Emma Martin Alterations** (1907) and **Garage** (1907)
Oak Park, Illinois

Several elements—masonry-like treatment of plaster walls,
lack of clarity in plan, among them—suggest a date earlier
than is generally given this structure. The building permit
was issued in 1901. Like the Heller (38), Husser (46), and
Rollin Furbeck (44) houses, it is a three-story dwelling.
The house was a collaboration with Webster Tomlinson.
Six years after its construction, alterations were made for
Emma Martin, and a garage, in the style of the house, added
(visible at far left in photograph). For many years it was
known as the Emma Martin house.

61 William E. Martin Residence (1902)
Oak Park, Illinois

The plaster and wood trim of this three-story dwelling for
W. E. Martin, brother of Darwin D. Martin—see E-Z Polish
Factory (114) and other Martin listings (100-102, 225,
226)—is not too unlike that of the Fricke residence (58).
Yet it is closer to the Prairie ideal, as typified by the Willits
Residence (54), being much clearer in plan. The building
had been, for several years, subdivided into three apart-
ments when, in 1945, it was restored to single-family usage.

62, 62A   **River Forest Golf Club** (1898) and **Addition** (1901)
River Forest, Illinois
Demolished

This building was a single-story structure of horizontal
board and batten construction, originally of T plan. In
1901 it was considerably enlarged in the top of the T by
extension and addition of an octagonal lounge. The photograph shows the original structure, before enlargement.

63 Universal Portland Cement Company, **Buffalo Exposition Pavilion** (1901)
Buffalo, New York
Demolished

Though the Universal Portland Cement Company never commissioned a permanent building from Wright, it did commission this work for the 1901 Pan American Exposition in Buffalo and an exhibition in Madison Square Garden in 1910 (163). Neither photographs nor plan seem to have survived the structure.

(64) T. E. Wilder Stable (1901)
Elmhurst, Illinois

This structure is by Webster Tomlinson's draftsman, Walter Burley Griffin, though Wright may have been partially involved in its design.

65, 66 Edward C. **Waller Gates** and **Stables** (1901)
River Forest, Illinois
Stables demolished

All that remains of the work done for Edward Waller by Wright are his two apartment buildings (30, 31) and these gates to Auvergne Place, where he was neighbor of William Winslow. The house in Auvergne Place that Wright remodeled for Waller has been demolished. Of the gates, the stonework remains, but lighting fixtures and ironwork are gone.

67 Frank Wright **Thomas** Residence, "The Harem" (1901)
Oak Park, Illinois

The first Prairie style house in Oak Park, the Thomas residence was long known in a version surfaced with shingles. Restoration to the original plaster surface was begun in 1975 by the Robert D. Colemans. Commissioned by James C. Rogers, it was given to his daughter and son-in-law, Mr. and Mrs. Frank Thomas, upon completion. Its L plan was probably the idea of Walter Burley Griffin, who came to Wright through his collaboration with Webster Tomlinson.

68 E. Arthur **Davenport** Residence (1901)
River Forest, Illinois

This is a straightforward two-story, gable-roofed, stained-wood board and batten structure, with plaster under the eaves. A front terrace has been removed. The house was done in collaboration with Webster Tomlinson.

69 Nell and Jane Lloyd Jones, **Hillside Home School II** (1901)
Spring Green, Wisconsin

Hillside (the school building proper is on the right in the
photograph) has gone through many transformations. The
first building, dating from 1887 (1), was demolished in
1950. The second school was built in 1903 for Wright's
aunts. With the formation of the Taliesin Fellowship in
1933, the school became a part of that complex. It has
since undergone considerable remodeling and the left
section (in the photograph) dates from these more recent
times. The interior is of H plan, and materials include native
limestone, oak, and plaster.

The remodeling of the building since 1933 is listed as part
of a separate project: Frank Lloyd Wright, **Taliesin Fellowship Complex** (228).

70 Francis W. **Little** (Little-Clarke) **Residence I** and
71 **Stable** (1902)
Peoria, Illinois

The first Little residence is a brick home of T plan with a
separate, large stable. Additions were completed by Wright
in 1909 for Robert Clarke (152). The porch has since been
enclosed with glass. The Littles also built a "Northome" in
Minnesota a decade later (173).

72 Susan Lawrence **Dana Residence** (1902) and
73 **Lawrence Memorial Library** (1905)
Springfield, Illinois

The Dana residence, of cruciform plan, incorporates an earlier house into its Prairie style brick structure. It is the first
example of Wright's work to feature a two-story-high living
room. Sculptor Richard Bock and the Linden Glass Company, regular collaborators with Wright in this period, contributed to the design. Though the designs for details are
abstract patterns, they derive largely from prairie sumac.
The Lawrence Memorial Library (at the left in the photograph) is connected to the main structure by a raised walkway.

74 Arthur **Heurtley Residence** (1902)
Oak Park, Illinois

In 1902 Arthur Heurtley commissioned two works, a home half a block away from Wright's studio and a cottage in northern Michigan (75). In this home Roman brick is laid so that, at a distance, it suggests board and batten. The plan is square, and living quarters are above ground in typical Prairie fashion. It has been remodeled into two apartments.

75 Arthur **Heurtley Summer Residence Remodeling** (1902)
Marquette Island, Michigan

The Heurtley cottage was only a remodeling. Exterior walls
lean inwards, much as the George Smith house (45). Horizontal siding, originally stained, is now painted. The large
living room and its dominating fireplace are clearly Wrightian touches. The building is one of many cottages on the
properties of Les Cheneaux Club. It has been altered with
glass in place of screen, and a balcony has been added on
the south side of the western facade (side opposite to that
shown in the photograph). Below the hillside lakefront retreat is a boathouse with similar exterior treatment, perhaps by Wright but not authenticated.

76 E. H. **Pitkin** Residence (1900)
Sapper Island, Desbarats, Ontario, Canada

Wright built several cottages in this period. The Pitkin residence, one of the first, is near the Heurtley cottage by boat,
though some distance via Sault Sainte Marie and ground
transportation. Designed as a "Swiss chalet," it is located
on the westernmost promontory of Sapper Island. Pitkin
visited the area on a summer cruise, apparently expecting to
find a thriving colony of vacationers. Few were there, but
on a side cruise he found this lovely location with an incom-
parable view of northern sunsets. Many nearby cottages reveal the influence of this Wright work in their copying of
roof lines and board and batten construction. The cottage
has been altered over the years, mostly, it seems, on the exterior. The living room and stone fireplace retain their
Wrightian character.

77 George Gerts Double House, "Bridge Cottage" (1902)
Whitehall, Michigan

Birch Brook flows under the bridged loggia of this T-plan
(double-L) cottage and fifty yards farther empties into
White Lake. South Shore Drive is well above the cottage,
which is entered halfway down a steep hill. Once a wall
divided the T into two Ls. Each L had its own fireplace,
though they shared a common chimney. Now, with the
wall removed, they are back to back and jut into the top
of the T somewhat anachronistically.

78 Walter Gerts Residence (1902)
Whitehall, Michigan
Mostly demolished

This structure has been relocated on the lot, resurfaced,
and gutted. The original was a single-story board and batten
structure of rectangular plan, with centrally located fireplace.

79 Henry **Wallis** (Wallis-Goodsmith) **Summer Residence** (1900)
80 and **Boathouse** (1897)
Lake Delavan, Wisconsin
Boathouse demolished

Five summer residences (79, 81, 82, 83, 87), all part of a
Delavan Lake group, may have been designed and built in
fewer years than the dates commonly assigned to them
indicate. Wright was supervising construction of at least the
Fred Jones (83) and A. P. Johnson (87) structures at the
same time. The Wallis cottage was unsupervised and sold
upon completion to H. Goodsmith. Horizontal board and
batten siding has been mostly resurfaced.

81 George W. Spencer Residence (1902)
Lake Delavan, Wisconsin

Wright supposedly disowned the George Spencer cottage
when, during construction, it was altered so that the boards
on the second level were laid vertically.

82 Charles S. Ross Residence (1902)
Lake Delavan, Wisconsin

The Charles Ross cottage is a cruciform-plan, board and batten, Prairie style structure, originally stained dark, now painted yellow. The first-story veranda has been enclosed and the second story extended and enclosed. This latter alteration considerably increased upper floor space and made that story symmetrical about two axes, modifying its original T plan.

83, 84 **Fred B. Jones Residence, Gate Lodge,**
85, 86 **Barn with Stables,** and **Boathouse,**
"Penwern" (1903)
Lake Delavan, Wisconsin

This is the most extensive of the Delavan Lake Projects. The arches at the porte-cochere and front veranda distinguish it from all the other lakeside cottages. The main house has a living room the width of the lake facade, and the stair therein leads to a balcony that opens over living, dining, and other rooms. It features a large Roman brick fireplace; rooms and new woodwork have been added. Exterior is board and batten siding. The gate lodge is directly on South Shore Road, and the boathouse sits so that only the roof rises to the brow of the hill. The work was only partially supervised by Wright.

Fred B. Jones Boathouse

87 A. P. Johnson Residence (1905)
Lake Delavan, Wisconsin

It is said that when Wright, approaching on horseback via the
the dirt driveway to supervise final stages of work on this
Prairie style tongue-and-groove-sided house, saw it painted
white, he rode away, never to return. As of 1970, restoration of the house, which still retains its fine leaded windows
and Roman brick fireplace, by owner Robert Wright (no relation to the architect) was underway. By 1971, when this
photograph was taken, landscaping had been considerably
improved, and modernization of the kitchen was completed.
The building is to be given a darker exterior and may then,
for the first time in its history, look as its architect intended.

88   **Mrs. Thomas H. Gale Summer Residence,**
89, 90   **Summer Residence Duplicate I and II (1905)**
Whitehall, Michigan
Duplicate II mostly demolished

Another board and batten cottage, this summer house has an almost flat roofline. The dating is not certain, and the work was unsupervised. Two other nearly identical units were erected on lots nearby, each set differently to take advantage of its site. Only one duplicate remains in good condition, and it was renovated in 1970-1971. The original is dark green, Duplicate I dark brown, and Duplicate II white.

91 J. J. **Walser**, Jr. Residence (1903)
Chicago, Illinois

This Prairie style house of wood with plaster surface now stands in rather cramped quarters, between apartment buildings. There have been alterations to the rear of the structure.

(92) W. H. Freeman Residence (1903)
Hinsdale, Illinois

Though this work has been commonly listed among
Wright's completed oeuvre, no evidence, photographic or
otherwise, has come forth to prove that it was constructed.
Photographs do show a structure, on the lot across from the
Abbott House by William Drummond, different from that
designed by Wright.

93 Larkin Company Administration **Building** (1903)
Buffalo, New York
Demolished, 1949-1950

The Larkin Company was a mail-order business. Among
the firsts of the Larkin Building are use of air conditioning
and plate glass. Also, the furniture was of metal. Wright
entrusted the working drawings of the project to William
Drummond, many of whose own designs were constructed
near Wright works, often causing the casual viewer confusion about which is which (see Isabel Roberts, 150, and
Coonley residence, 135). Larkin Company cofounders were
John Larkin and Elbert Hubbard (one of whose sisters was
Mrs. Larkin). All the Wright homeowners in Buffalo were
involved with this enterprise in some manner. Darwin D.
Martin (see 100-102, 114, 225, 226) replaced Hubbard on
the latter's retirement. Alexander Davidson (149) was a
Larkin Company advertising manager. W. R. Heath (105)
was an attorney for the Larkin enterprise. George Barton
(103) married Martin's daughter.

94 Scoville Park Fountain (1903)
Oak Park, Illinois

In an article by Donald P. Hallmark in the Second Quarter 1971 *Prairie School Review*, this work is identified, not as "with sculpture by Richard Bock," but as by Bock "with the help of Wright." As Bock's work, it is known as the Horse Show Fountain and was dedicated on July 24, 1909. This listing, however, attributing the work to Wright from a much earlier year, agrees with the records of the Frank Lloyd Wright Foundation. The current work is a replica of the fountain, with new sculpture that is an interpretation of Bock's original work.

95 Reverend Mr. Jenkin Lloyd Jones, **Abraham Lincoln Center** (1903)
Chicago, Illinois

The original project, for All Souls Church, had more of Wright's signature on it than this construction. The first-floor lobby reveals the imprint of Wright, but the building may be largely attributed to, and was entirely executed by, Dwight Heald Perkins. John Lloyd Wright claims the original design to have been his father's first architectural work and dates it 1888. Intended for use as a community center, it was built in 1903 in Perkins's altered form.

96 Unity Church (1904)
Oak Park, Illinois

Unity Church is the first significant American architectural statement in poured concrete. Wright's use of concrete is truly original, making no obeisance to earlier French experiments in this material. With its exposed pebble surface, the Unity monolith introduced reinforced-concrete construction to America on a grand scale. Its use was dictated in part by the need to keep costs of the structure low; only $35,000 was available to house a congregation of 400 persons. Unity Church is composed of what Wright called Unity Temple— the north section (on the left in the photograph), whose plan inscribes a Greek cross in a square, used for religious services—and Unity House, the parish house to the south. The prime mover in the building committee that chose Wright as architect was Charles Roberts (see 40, 41). The working drawings were prepared by Barry Byrne, who, after leaving Wright's office, became one of the more successful and imaginative of Prairie School architects. Renovations, begun in 1962, have continued over the years, although they are limited by available funds. Visitors' donations help the work progress. The church is open daily to the public. This structure has been designated by the American Institute of Architects as one of seventeen American buildings designed by Frank Lloyd Wright to be retained as an example of his architectural contribution to American culture.

97 Robert M. **Lamp Residence** (1904)
Madison, Wisconsin

At one time this was a simple rectangular brick structure
bearing some semblance to Unity Church (96) in principle.
A third story, totally out of keeping with Wright's concept,
has been added, and the brick painted white. Had the brick
been concrete, the relationship to Unity Church and also to
the Mrs. Thomas H. Gale Residence (98) would be more
apparent.

98 Mrs. Thomas H. Gale Residence (1904)
Oak Park, Illinois

If the date on a perspective drawing is good evidence, this
design dates from 1904 or earlier, before the Robie house
(127) and approximately the same time as Unity Church
(96) and the Lamp residence (97). The commonly accepted
date, 1909, is that of const. uction. Roughly square in plan,
with concrete originally envisioned as the construction material, this plaster-surfaced, wood-trimmed Prairie house is
often suggested as the spiritual progenitor of Fallingwater
(230). In its use of cantilever design, it does anticipate
Fallingwater, yet the Gale house is itself the offspring of the
1902 Yahara Boat Club Project, which gave birth to nearly
all the flat-roofed Prairie houses by Wright. The Yahara
landmark in Wright's inventive thought was never built.

99 Burton J. **Westcott** Residence (1904)
Springfield, Ohio
Dating of this house is not certain, although in Springfield
it is put at 1904. It is one of the larger of the square-plan
Prairie style wood houses with plaster surface.

Buffalo, New York
Garage and Conservatory demolished

Darwin D. Martin was a brother of W. E. Martin (61); they
were partners in the E-Z Polish Factory (114). In Buffalo
Darwin Martin assumed Elbert Hubbard's administrative
duties when that cofounder of the Larkin Company (93)
retired. This house, with its conservatory and connecting
gallery, was originally the largest expression of the T plan
in a Prairie style house. Primary construction materials are
russet Roman brick and oak. Orlando Gianinni, often associated with Wright in this period, did the glass work. Garage
and conservatory with gallery have been demolished, and
apartment buildings now crowd the lot.

103 George **Barton** Residence (1903)
Buffalo, New York

Mrs. Barton was the sister of Darwin D. Martin, and the
Barton dwelling was built on space immediately adjacent to
the north limit of the Martin residence (100) as originally
constructed with gallery and conservatory. The cruciform
plan is articulated on the main floor by western dining and
eastern living rooms, northern kitchen, and southern entry
and veranda. The house is being restored by Eric Larrabee
and his architect wife, Eleanor Larrabee.

104 Edwin H. **Cheney** Residence (1903)
Oak Park, Illinois

This is a single-story house in brick with wood trim. A brick wall encloses its terrace. Mamah Borthwick Cheney, wife of Edwin Cheney, accompanied Wright to Europe when the architect left America for a year in 1909; she later died in a fire that destroyed Taliesin.

105 W. R. **Heath** Residence (1905)
Buffalo, New York

Although 1905 is the year of Wright's first visit to Japan,
the effect of what he saw there is not apparent in this work.
The Heath dwelling is a dark red brick Prairie style structure
with large eastern porch and a living room opening to the
southern sky that breaks the rectangle into a stubby T plan.
Mr. Heath was attorney to the Larkin Company (93), and
his wife was a sister of Elbert Hubbard, cofounder of the
Larkin mail-order enterprise.

106 Harvey P. **Sutton** Residence (1905)
McCook, Nebraska

Wright's only work in Nebraska, the Sutton residence is a plaster-surfaced, wood-trimmed Prairie style structure. The building housed a doctor's offices in the early 1970s.

107   Hiram **Baldwin** Residence (1905)
Kenilworth, Illinois

A Prairie style house, which has been remodeled extensively
inside, the Baldwin residence is located on a large north corner lot.

108 Mary M. W. Adams Residence (1905)
Highland Park, Illinois

This is a plaster-surfaced, wood-frame Prairie style house
located on a southeast corner lot near Lake Michigan. Its
best face (left side in the photograph) is turned away from
public view.

109 W. A. **Glasner** Residence (1905)
Glencoe, Illinois

Situated on a brow of a ravine, this house defies simple designation as to plan type, though its major axis is east-west
and all spaces flow from this spine. It features organization
of spaces similar to later Usonian designs in that no separate
room was planned just for dining. Although the original
plan included a bridge over one part of the ravine, that extension was never built. Like many Prairie style houses with
horizontal board and batten exteriors, the wood is rough
sawn in finish. Many remodelings of Wright houses wrongly
use smooth lumber under the mistaken notion that this
original rough wood was used for economy; in fact, it was
often preferred by the architect. The Glasner dwelling was
renovated in 1926 and 1938 and is undergoing restoration
by Dr. and Mrs. Henry Fineberg in 1972-1973. The west
porch has been enclosed, and the east library (left in the
photograph) was enlarged, one side eliminating the octagonal plan, in an earlier renovation.

110 Charles E. Brown Residence (1905)
Evanston, Illinois

A compact rectangle, with open front porch, in horizontal
board and batten, the Charles Brown house also has plaster
under the eaves and between top-story windows. Note the
double-hung windows, rare among Wright's contemporary
designs and previously noted with respect to the Winslow
house (24).

111 Frank L. Smith Bank, First National Bank of Dwight (1905)
Dwight, Illinois

The cut-stone exterior conceals the Wrightian delineation of interior spaces. The building was completely renovated in 1970. It is open during regular banking hours.

112 E. W. **Cummings Real Estate Office** (1905)
River Forest, Illinois
Demolished

Two photographs, one shown here, constitute most of the
knowledge we have of this structure. A Prairie structure of
wood and plaster with broad overhanging eaves, it was surrounded by an imposingly high wall and gates framed by
urns of Wright's design. (Photograph by William G. Purcell.)

113 **Rookery Building** Entryway and Lobby **Remodeling** (1905)
Chicago, Illinois

In the late 1890s Wright, the American Luxfer Prism Company (which contracted lighting fixtures designed by Wright), and William Winslow (24) all had offices in this building, which was under the management of another Wright client and patron, Edward C. Waller (see 30, 31, 47, 65, 66). Wright remodeled only the entryway and lobby in this 1886 skyscraper by Burnham and Root. There have been further alterations since Wright's work. The building is open during regular business hours.

114 Darwin D. Martin and W. E. Martin, **E-Z Polish Factory**
(1905)
Chicago, Illinois

This building, designed for the Martin brothers (see 61,
100-102) as a polish-making factory, now serves other
commercial uses. Upper floors were rebuilt after a 1913
fire, and most of the windows have been bricked in. One
painted mural survives on the main office floor.

115 Thomas P. **Hardy** Residence (1905)
Racine, Wisconsin

It seems that few people view the Hardy house as Wright envisioned it (as shown in a penned drawing in Japanese style
from his own, or Marion Mahony's hand) from the Lake
Michigan shoreline. The photograph here published reveals
that lakeside aspect. The terrace is one story below street
level, and the living room, with its upper-story balcony,
opens the entire living quarters to the Lake Michigan view.
None of this is apparent from the street (western) approach.

116 W. H. **Pettit Mortuary Chapel** (1906)
Belvidere, Illinois

The chapel is a T-plan, one-story, plaster-surfaced, wooden "Prairie Mortuary Chapel"; the Belvidere Cemetery is open at all times.

117 P. A. **Beachy** Residence (1906)
Oak Park, Illinois

Of brick and plaster with wood trim, the Beachy residence,
like the 1902 Dana house (72), incorporates an earlier
house into its structure. Barry Byrne was involved in preparation of working drawings and supervision.

118 Frederick **Nicholas** Residence (1906)
Flossmoor, Illinois

A stained, lapped wood siding cube, the Nicholas house was
not supervised by Wright during construction.

119 River Forest Tennis Club (1906)
River Forest, Illinois
On this horizontal board and batten project, Charles E.
White and Vernon S. Watson were associated with Wright.
Watson later added to and otherwise altered the structure.
It was moved from its original site in 1920. Today it re-
veals but little of Wright's contribution.

120 P. D. **Hoyt** Residence (1906)
Geneva, Illinois

A square-plan, Prairie style house, the Hoyt residence has a plastered surface and stained wood trim. Mrs. Hoyt was a daughter of Colonel George Fabyan (129).

121, 122   A. W. **Gridley Residence** and **Barn** (1906)
Batavia, Illinois
Barn demolished

This Prairie style house of plastered surface and stained
wood trim is of cruciform plan on the ground floor and T
plan at the second story, which has no upper level at the
long, open porch.

123 Grace Fuller Residence (1906)
Glencoe, Illinois
Demolished

The second house designed by Wright in Glencoe (after the
Glasner, 109), this was a design of two-story square plan,
the lower floor extended by a wing. This small Prairie house
was plaster surfaced and wood trimmed. (Rendering by
Harvey Ferrero.)

124   C. Thaxter **Shaw** Residence **Remodeling** (1906)
Montreal, Quebec, Canada
Demolished

Although Wright designed a residence for Shaw, the only work by Wright that was completed for this client was a small amount of remodeling in a row house complex. Continual alterations have totally obscured Wright's work.

125   K. C. **DeRhodes** Residence (1906)
South Bend, Indiana

The wood-trimmed, plaster-surfaced Prairie style DeRhodes residence now houses a club. The main floor features an immense living room, now an assembly room, that spans the entire length of the building. The side entryways turn this otherwise plain rectangle into a cruciform plan.

126 George Madison **Millard** Residence (1906)
Highland Park, Illinois

This is a two-story, cruciform-plan, board and batten Prairie style structure. Seventeen years later, Mrs. Millard built "La Miniatura" in Pasadena, California (214).

127 Frederick C. **Robie** Residence (1906)
Chicago, Illinois

The Robie house, as Wright's best expression of the Prairie masonry structure, is a national landmark. It has been designated by the AIA as one of seventeen American buildings designed by Frank Lloyd Wright to be retained as an example of his architectural contribution to American culture. Sheathed in Roman brick and overhung so perfectly that a midsummer noon sun barely strikes the foot of the long, glass-walled southern explosure of the raised above-ground-level living quarters, it demonstrates Wright's total control and appreciation of microclimatic effects. This is coupled with a high degree of integration of the mechanical and electrical systems designed by Wright into the visual expression of the interior. Living and dining space are in-line, with only the fireplace-chimney block providing separation (a plan, revealing this arrangement, may be found near the back of this book). Sleeping quarters are yet a floor above, play and billiard rooms below; there is no "basement." Construction was begun in 1908 and completed the following year. The garage and its surrounding wall were later altered from the original design. The building's local nickname, "The Battleship," has never gained currency among Wright scholars. Groups, upon advance arrangement, are permitted visits.

128 F. F. **Tomek** Residence (1907)
Riverside, Illinois

This Prairie plan has a small, second-story square centered over a large, main-floor L plan. Supports to the terrace roof are later additions. Barry Byrne drew the working drawings and was involved in construction supervision.

129 Colonel George **Fabyan** Game Preserve **Remodeling** (1907)
Geneva, Illinois

For Wright, one client invariably led to another. Wright designed the Hoyt house (120) in 1906, and this led to the Gridley commission (121, 122). While Wright was supervising construction of these two works, he met Colonel Fabyan, father of Mrs. Hoyt, who commissioned remodeling of two structures on his game preserve, one for a Fox River Country Club and the other a residence in the preserve (shown here), overlooking the Fox River. Remodeling included details of the main-floor living room, the north room of the second story, and some exterior work.

130 **Fox River Country Club Remodeling** (1907)
Geneva, Illinois
Demolished

This, like the Game Preserve remodeling for Colonel Fabyan
(129), was a reworking of an existing structure on the estates of the Colonel. It was destroyed by fire only a few
years after the remodeling was completed.

131 Pebbles & Balch Shop (1907)
Oak Park, Illinois
Demolished

This is actually a remodeling of a building on Lake Street
for Pebbles and Balch, interior decorators. It reveals the
influence of Wright's visit to Japan in both interior and
exterior. Inside, natural woods, oiled paper for glass, and
plain surfaces were seen side by side with lighting fixtures
of geometrical forms used by Wright for over a decade.
Wright also designed a home for O. B. Balch (168).

132   Larkin Company, Jamestown Exhibition Pavilion (1907)
Sewell Point, Norfolk, Virginia

This interesting structure was designed for construction in the Jamestown Tercentennial exhibition held, not at Jamestown, but on the seashore at Norfolk. The grounds have since been occupied by a naval base.

132   Darwin D. Martin Gardener's Cottage (1905)
Buffalo, New York

This house, near the Darwin D. Martin complex (100-102), avoids the russet Roman brick of its illustrious neighbor and turns to plaster on a wood frame. The overhang is not as broad as other Wright houses of this type, thus suggesting the possibility of its design by one of the draftsmen in Wright's employ, yet the plan seems to be Wright's. At the time of publication of the first edition of this catalog, these plans were not on the list of items in the Taliesin archives, and stylistic evidence argued against its inclusion. The rear of the structure has been altered by additions.

133 George **Blossom Garage** (1907)
Chicago, Illinois

To the rear of the Colonial Revival Blossom house (14) is
the much later Prairie style garage in Roman brick with
wood trim. Here Wright obviously ignored the original
house and designed in his then current Prairie style.

134 Andrew T. **Porter** Residence, "Tanyderi" (1907)
Spring Green, Wisconsin

Tanyderi—"under the oaks" in Welsh—was built for Wright's
sister Jane and brother-in-law on the grounds of Taliesin.
Siding is of shingles. Stylistic evidence suggests a design date
of 1901 or earlier, with construction being delayed until
1907, the date generally accepted for this work. By this
later date, Wright would have provided a design more in
keeping with Prairie style ideas; perhaps this explains why
the architect on occasion denied that the design was his.

135, 136 Avery **Coonley Residence** (1907), **Gardener's Cottage**
137 (1911), and **Coach House** (1911)
Riverside, Illinois

The Coonley residence provides the first example in Wright's
work of the zoned plan. Living quarters are raised, in typical Prairie fashion, and a pavilion links various spaces. Inlaid
tiles form a geometrical pattern in the frieze on the plaster-
surfaced, wood-trimmed house. Published plans (actual
working drawings were by Barry Byrne) include the cottage
and coach house, originally a stable, so their design date
might also be set at 1907, but construction was well after
the 1909 completion of the main residential structure. The
entire project has been somewhat altered, the residence
being converted into three separate apartments. The coach
house and contiguous sunken gardens are now a separate
plot. Remodeling of the stable into the coach house was the
late 1950s work of Arnold P. Skow for Carolyn and James
W. Howlett. On the corner opposite the former Coonley estate is "Thorncroft," one of the finest examples of Prairie
school architecture by an early Wright apprentice, William
Drummond.

Coonley Gardener's Cottage and Coach House

138 Stephen M. B. **Hunt Residence I** (1907)
La Grange, Illinois

This is the best-constructed example of "A Fireproof House of $5000" from the April 1907 *Ladies Home Journal*. Originally planned for construction in concrete, which would have made it fireproof, it is a square-plan, Prairie style building in wood and plaster. The terraces have been enclosed. Restoration over the past decade has been undertaken by Edward M. Marcisz. The Tiffany brick fireplace and oak woodwork have been fully restored. (Photograph courtesy of Edward M. Marcisz.)

139 G. C. **Stockman** Residence (1908)
Mason City, Iowa

The Stockman house is Wright's first extant work in Iowa. Its design is basically that of the "Fireproof House of $5000" (138).

140 Robert W. **Evans** Residence (1908)
Chicago, Illinois

From a basic square, this Prairie structure extends into a
cruciform plan, with porch on the south (left in photograph) balancing porte-cochere on the north. It has been
resurfaced with a stone veneer and otherwise altered.

141 Browne's Bookstore (1908)
Chicago, Illinois
Demolished

The placement and limited height of bookshelves created alcoves around tables, each with four Wright-designed chairs, providing the cosy atmosphere desired in the bookstore setting.

142 L. K. **Horner** Residence (1908)
Chicago, Illinois
Demolished

Published photographs reveal a strong kinship between the Horner and Mrs. Thomas H. Gale (98) residences.

143 Willard Ashton, **Horseshoe Inn** (1908)
Estes Park, Colorado
Demolished

Little is known of this structure, though it is likely of the
same genre as the Como Orchard Summer Colony project
(144).

144 Como Orchard Summer Colony (1908)
University Heights, Darby, Montana
Mostly demolished

One small Land Office building and one altered cottage are
all that remain of the Como Orchard (Land Company)
Summer Colony project. Apparently a speculative and rec-
reational proposal for University of Chicago professors and
other vacationers, it never grew beyond the main inn
(shown in the photograph) and several cottages. Supervision
may have been by William Drummond and Marion Mahony.

145 Bitter Root Inn (1908)
Stevensville, Montana
Demolished by fire, July 28, 1924

This inn was to have been part of a complex of structures in
the Bitter Root Irrigation District. Though houses still in
the area show Prairie School influence, none has been spe-
cifically attributed to any of the major Chicago architects
of the period. Frederick Nicholas was a promoter of this
and the Como Orchard (144) projects, in which Wright may
also have invested.

146 E. A. **Gilmore** Residence, "Airplane House" (1908)
Madison, Wisconsin

The small porches of the Gilmore residence represent a break with Wright's rather consistent rectangular and octagonal modules.

147 E. E. **Boynton** Residence (1908)
Rochester, New York

A very elongated T plan of Prairie style surfaced with plaster and wood trim, the Boynton residence has been kept in good condition. Porches emphasize the elongation of the top of the T. Boynton knew of Wright through Warren McArthur, his partner in the Ham Lantern Company (see 11-13, 221, 222). Wright often visited the site during the year of construction, taking great care with details. He designed all of the furniture for the house and required that 28 elm trees be added to the plot. Barry Byrne, often entrusted with major projects such as Unity Church (96), prepared the working drawings.

148 Meyer **May** Residence (1908)
Grand Rapids, Michigan

The details in the May house, particularly the leaded ceiling windows, are most worthy of note. Roman brick is used throughout, including the 1920 rear extension that emphasizes the T plan. Window detailing is copper sheathed. Terrace and second-story porch are now enclosed.

149 Alexander **Davidson** Residence (1908)
Buffalo, New York

A Prairie style structure whose two-story living room faces
east, the Davidson house is of cruciform plan. Davidson was
the advertising manager appointed by Darwin Martin at the
Larkin Company (93).

150 Isabel Roberts (Roberts-Scott) Residence (1908)
River Forest, Illinois

This is a Prairie style house with a two-story-high living room, designed for Isabel Roberts, a bookkeeper of five years' standing in Wright's Oak Park Studio and daughter of Charles E. Roberts (40, 41). The original structure was of wood with plaster surface and, like the Baker (151) and Davidson (149) houses, of cruciform plan. It is a "split-level" dwelling, with living room at ground level, sleeping quarters a half-level above, and work spaces a half-level below. Wright remodeled the house for Warren Scott in 1955. Resurfacing was with brick veneer (as shown in the photograph), and blonde Philippine mahogany was used throughout the interior. The living room clerestory (center of photograph) starts only after an interrupting section of wall next to the floor-to-ceiling front windows (at left). The south porch is built around a tree that rises through the roofing. Immediately to the south and across the street are houses by a Prairie school disciple, William Drummond, who prepared the working drawings for the Isabel Roberts house.

151 Frank J. **Baker** Residence (1909)
Wilmette, Illinois

A Prairie style wood house with plaster surface, the Baker
dwelling also features a two-story-high living room. Its once-
open porches are now enclosed. The Baker living room
clerestory starts immediately from the floor-to-ceiling front
windows. The ground floor is cruciform, the second story
L plan, with no second story over either east or west porch.

152 Robert **Clarke Additions** to the **Little Residence I** (1909)
Peoria, Illinois
The Clarke additions elongated the original T plan of the
first Little residence (70). Published plans show the house
as enlarged.

153 Oscar **Steffens** Residence (1909)
Chicago, Illinois
Demolished
The Steffens residence was a two-story, cruciform-plan
Prairie style structure, with a two-story-high living room;
it was located near Lake Michigan.

154 Thurber Art Gallery (1909)
Chicago, Illinois
Demolished

Two long panels of leaded glass lighted the Thurber Art
Gallery on sunny days and concealed the indirect lighting
that lighted the gallery at other times. As in other "shops"
of this time, such as the Pebbles & Balch Shop (131) and
Browne's Bookstore (141), Wright took great care in achieving interesting interior spaces.

Mason City, Iowa
Law offices remodeling demolished

This bank and the Park Inn hotel behind it are now so thoroughly altered by store window fronts cut into the lower wall and other "modernizing" alterations as to disguise the once-elegant quality of these works. The project was nearly two years in construction and was completed by William Drummond during Wright's 1910 absence from America. J. E. E. Markley, whose eldest daughter had been a student at Wright's aunts' Hillside Home School I (1) in Spring Green, Wisconsin, probably brought Wright the commission. Had Wright not run off to Europe, Markley's business partner, James E. Blythe, might have become the kind of client that so often failed to materialize for the architect, one with many commissions at his command. Blythe and Markley were involved in the 1912 Rock Crest-Rock Glen project, designed by Walter Burley Griffin. Blythe built a Griffin-designed house and commissioned several others, including one for Arthur Rule of the law firm of Blythe, Markley, Rule and Smith. Wright had also designed at this time a house similar to Isabel Roberts's for J. C. Melson; Melson built a Griffin design. William Drummond and Barry Byrne also designed houses that were built in or near the Rock Glen area. But as these former Wright students were becoming independent of their master, the master himself was breaking free of his own past and looking westward in the second decade of the century for his future in architecture.

158   William H. **Copeland Residence Alterations** (1909) and
159   **Garage** (1908)
Oak Park, Illinois

The date on the plan from which Dr. Copeland's house was
remodeled is given as 1909. Downstairs, the three main
rooms and stairwell were extensively changed by Wright.
Outside, his handiwork may be recognized in the dormer
and roof, though other work, such as that at the porch and
entrance, is less easily identified. The garage, to the rear of
the lot, is clearly of Prairie style, consistent with the latter
part of the first decade of this century.

Copeland Garage

160 George C. **Stewart** Residence (1909)
Montecito, California

The first of the California houses, the Stewart house reveals
Wright's use of Midwestern Prairie concepts on the Pacific
Coast—two-story living room, broad overhanging roof, and
raised living quarters. The two-story-high living room is the
main feature of the structure. The living room and the
house plan suggest a board and batten reworking of the
Isabel Roberts house (150). Additions, not by Wright, have
been made to the west facade (on the right in the photograph).

161 J. Kibben **Ingalls** Residence (1909)
River Forest, Illinois

This square-plan Prairie style house of plastered surface and painted wood trim is Wright's last extant work in River Forest.

162 Peter C. **Stohr Arcade Building** (1909)
Chicago, Illinois
Demolished, December 1922

This building was located at the Wilson Avenue Station of
the Chicago "El." Most of it was under the "El" tracks—the
structure incorporated stairs to the ticket booths and rail-
way—but where it ducked out from under this obstruction,
it rose to three stories. The main-level row of shops extended the predominantly horizontal motif from the three-
tiered section. Between the taking of the photograph, circa
1919, and demolition three years later, a corner addition
intruded upon Wright's rectilinearity. W. G. Young & Co.,
once Young and Johnson, became the Uptown Real Estate
Co. The photograph shows the main part of Wright's work
including some of the third tier. (Photograph courtesy of
the Chicago Historical Society, detail from photograph of
Wilson Avenue Station.)

163 Universal Portland Cement Company, **New York City Exhibition** (1910)
New York, New York
Demolished

The Universal Portland Cement Company never had Wright design them a permanent structure. He did, however, design two works, both for public fairs. The first was for the Pan American Exposition in Buffalo in 1901 (63), and the second was this New York City Exhibition, held in Madison Square Garden.

164 Reverend J. R. **Ziegler** Residence (1909)
Frankfort, Kentucky

Wright's only work in Kentucky, a square Prairie style structure, this building was not supervised during construction
by the architect. It is located a short distance from the state
capitol building.

165 E. P. **Irving** Residence (1909)
Decatur, Illinois

This dwelling and the Amberg (166) and Mueller (167) were
supervised by Herman V. Von Holst and Marion Mahony
(later Mrs. Walter Burley Griffin) while Wright was traveling
outside America. How much of these houses is by Wright,
and how much by Mahony (who was the primary designing
influence in Wright's office during his absence) is not defi-
nitely known. In the Irving house, it would appear that the
exterior and plan are by Wright, with much of the interior
work by Mahony. The furniture for the three houses (165-
167) was by George M. Niedecken, long an associate of
Wright's in these matters.

166 J. H. **Amberg** Residence (1909)
Grand Rapids, Michigan

Though the final plan, finished while Wright was away from America, states this as a design of Von Holst and Mahony, Wright claimed the design as his. The proportions of the building suggest his hand in the plan and basic exterior design, while the handiwork of Marion Mahony is clearly evident in the interior treatment of living and dining spaces. The house is now divided into three apartments.

167 Robert **Mueller** Residence (1909)
Decatur, Illinois

This house, immediately east of the Irving residence (165),
may be the work of at least three designers, Wright, Marion
Mahony, and Walter Burley Griffin. Viewed next to the Irving
home, it looks too tall to be a true Wright design. Possibly
Wright completed the plan before leaving for Europe with
Mrs. Cheney. Then, when Marion Mahony found it difficult
to complete the design from plan alone, she may have con-
sulted Griffin (the man she later married), who had already
contributed to several Wright designs (67, perhaps 68).
Some works once attributed to the master have since been
credited to Griffin (see 64).

168 O. B. **Balch** Residence (1911)
Oak Park, Illinois

The current orangish tint of the wood trim and the gray
plaster provide contrast with the usual dark brown on white
of Wright's plaster-surfaced, wood-frame Prairie houses,
which was the original color pattern for this dwelling.
Wright also designed a shop for interior decorator Balch
(131).

169 Herbert **Angster** Residence (1911)
Lake Bluff, Illinois
Demolished

A Prairie house of plaster surface and wood trim, this
building was so densely surrounded by trees that good photographs were impossible to achieve. The George Madison
Millard residence (126) is located on a similarly wooded
site. Mrs. Angster was a sister-in-law of Sherman Booth
(187).

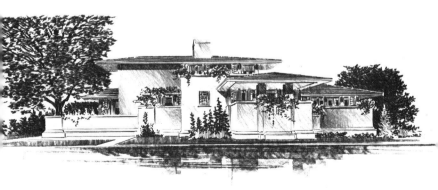

170 **Banff National Park Pavilion** (1911)
Alberta, Canada
Demolished, 1939

A very long, basically board and batten structure, this pa-
vilion was similar to the River Forest Tennis Club (119).
Wright worked in association with Francis C. Sullivan, a
Canadian architect.

171 Arthur L. Richards, **Geneva Inn** (1911)
Lake Geneva, Wisconsin
Demolished, 1970

This project was not completed as designed. A Prairie style
structure of wood frame as constructed, the main lobby
featured a large Roman brick fireplace. Dining and enter-
tainment facilities were west of the entry, guest rooms in
an east wing. Plain and identical, these rooms could have
allowed indefinite extension of this wing to accommodate
any number of guests. They faced south, to the sun and
Lake Geneva. A new high-rise apartment building of no dis-
tinction stood on the lot in mid-1971.

172 Frank Lloyd Wright, **Taliesin I** (1911)
Spring Green, Wisconsin
Demolished, 1914

Living quarters were destroyed by fire; other quarters survive in today's Taliesin III (218). Taliesin I was built on land of Wright's mother, Anna Lloyd Jones Wright, who lived for many years in Taliesins I and II. Taliesin I provided a haven for son Frank and Mamah Borthwick Cheney, wife of a former client (104), with whom the architect had gone to Europe in 1909.

173 Francis W. **Little Residence II**, "Northome" (1912)
Deephaven, Minnesota
Demolished, 1972 (living room to be reconstructed at Metropolitan Museum of Art, New York City)
Demolished, 1972 (living room reconstructed in the Metropolitan Museum of Art, New York City; library reconstructed in the Allentown Art Museum, Pennsylvania)

Wright's first building in Minnesota used its site most effectively. Overlooking Robinson Bay of Lake Minnetonka, the 55-foot living room, perhaps Wright's most spacious domestic interior from this Prairie period, opened its secondary view inland. Sleeping quarters were also on the main and upper floors, opposite the living room and over the dining space which nestled in a hilly depression. Two adjacent buildings, though of Prairie board and batten style, were not done by Wright. At the time of demolition, several museums removed sections for later reconstruction. The living room is in the American wing of the Metropolitan Museum of Art, New York City. The library now opens on to an enclosed courtyard at the Allentown Art Museum in eastern Pennsylvania.

Photo on overleaf

Little Residence II Living Room

174 Avery **Coonley Playhouse** (1912)
Riverside, Illinois

A post-Prairie symmetrical cruciform plan, this building has
been significantly altered by the glass enclosure of wing
spaces and removal of a small front flower-box wall. The
clerestory windows, in many-colored geometrical designs
by Wright, would deserve a detailed note if all were still
intact.

175 Park Ridge Country Club Remodeling (1912)
Park Ridge, Illinois
Demolished

Wright both added to and altered an existing building in his remodeling of the clubhouse of the Park Ridge Country Club.

176 William B. **Greene** Residence (1912)
Aurora, Illinois

Familiar elements are present here: plaster surface, wood
trim, hipped roof. Harry Robinson, Wright's draftsman, was
involved in the original drawings and supervision of construction and was called upon in 1926 to add a dining room
and master bedroom wing (on the right in the photograph).
The old screened porch was removed, and an enclosed,
heated porch added in 1961 by Robert Mall, for William A.
Greene, son of the original client.

(177) Florida Cottage (1912)
       Palm Beach, Florida

       Wright designed a single-story asymmetrical H-plan struc-
       ture for Palm Beach; it was not built. The client, William
       Koehne, like several others of this time, ended up using a
       design by Walter Burley Griffin. "Villa Zila" was a two-
       story structure at the beach; in later years it became the
       Shorewinds Motel. Attempts to save it, first as a Wright
       building, later correctly in Griffin's name, failed, and it was
       demolished in the mid-1970s.

(178) M. B. Hilly Residence (1913)
       Brookfield, Illinois

       A one-story, square-plan, board and batten bungalow, the
       building is thought to have been designed for Brookfield
       but may have been a cottage constructed on the eastern
       shore of Lake Michigan. The building has not been located
       in Brookfield. It may have been a summer cottage designed
       for Hilly while he was living in Illinois and built in south-
       west Michigan, where many Chicago-area residents vaca-
       tioned. Information obtained after publication of the first
       edition indicates that this item was not built.

179 **Harry S. Adams** Residence (1913)
Oak Park, Illinois

This large brick structure is Wright's last work in Oak Park and represents a summation of the Prairie style just as Wright is turning the page in his career to Midway Gardens and new ideas. Its longitudinal plan runs from porte-cochere through porch, living room and hall to dining room. All is set on a stylobate base under broad, hipped roofing, with casement windows and stained glass. Even the entry, behind the, by then ubiquitous, concrete flower pot (see 186 for a variation, 127 for the standard) is partially concealed.

180 Edward C. Waller, Jr., **Midway Gardens** (1913)
Chicago, Illinois
Demolished, 1929

Prohibition was but one of the many factors that destroyed
the Midway Gardens pleasure palace. Only two years after
being opened, it was purchased by the Edelweiss Brewing
Company and converted to serve the needs of a clientele
hardly accustomed to its refined surroundings. The richness
of architectural expression, in patterned concrete block and
brick, was exceptional. An entire city block was enclosed
by the structure, while the interior court was open to the
elements yet separated from the harshness of urban life.
Sculptures by Alfonzo Iannelli adorned the work, and John
Lloyd Wright, a son of the architect, assisted in construction supervision. Of the major nondomestic works of Wright
completed prior to the Johnson Administration Building
(237)—The Larkin Company Administration Building (93),
Midway Gardens, the Imperial Hotel (194), and Unity
Church (96)—only the last-named exists today.

181 **Mori Oriental Art Studio** (1914)
Chicago, Illinois
Demolished

The southeast corner room on the eighth floor of the Fine
Arts Building on Michigan Avenue is quite large with a high
ceiling. Wright decorated this interior for use as an art studio, much along the lines of other small commercial enter-
prises, such as Browne's Bookstore (141), the Pebbles &
Balch Shop (131), and the Thurber Art Gallery (154). The
characteristic feature of Wright's work was the geometrical
lighting fixtures, of which similar types can be seen in the
interior photographs of Browne's Bookstore and the Pebbles
& Balch Shop and also the Rookery Building Remodeling
(113). Though the Fine Arts Building still stands, Wright's
work has long since been removed.

182 Frank Lloyd Wright, **Taliesin II** (1914)
Spring Green, Wisconsin
Demolished, 1925

Only living quarters were destroyed by fire, while other
quarters remain today from Taliesin I (172).

183 A. D. **German Warehouse** (1915)
Richland Center, Wisconsin

Though Wright was born in Richland Center, it was 48
years before a design of his was erected there. When it did
come, it was this imposing cube of brick and cast-in-place
concrete, a warehouse. Two-thirds of the main floor space
is open for storage, obstructed only by widely-spaced
columns. Finely patterned block faces the top story, which
was reserved for cold storage. This structure, never fully
completed, is now the Richland Museum.

184 E. D. **Brigham** Residence (1915)
Glencoe, Illinois

One of seven houses in Glencoe designed by Wright during this year, this is the only one not part of Sherman Booth's concern (185-192). Wright did not supervise construction, and many alterations in both materials and design details were made without his consent.

185-192 Sherman M. Booth, **Ravine Bluffs Development**

185, 186 **Ravine Bluffs Development Sculptures** and **Bridge** (1915)
Glencoe, Illinois

Sherman M. Booth commissioned a complete plan for a housing development just west of a Glencoe ravine. Six homes, including his own, were built. Additionally, there are several sculptures (one of which is shown here) in poured concrete. These were probably executed by Alfonzo Iannelli, collaborator with Wright in the early part of this decade on several projects, including the Midway Gardens (180). The northeastern entrance to the development is by way of a bridge over the ravine from which the project takes its name. Three lots south is the honeymoon cottage for Sylvan Booth, relocated from its original location near the Sherman Booth house (187), and once claimed by a Chicago newspaper to be by Wright. It is not listed here for lack of sufficient evidence of authenticity.

Ravine Bluffs Development Sculpture

Ravine Bluffs Development Bridge

Ravine Bluffs Development
187 Sherman M. **Booth Residence** (1915)
Glencoe, Illinois

Booth was Wright's lawyer at this time. He commissioned
the Ravine Bluffs Development, but his own house is not as
extensive or fanciful as that first planned by Wright. That
idea included a bridge spanning the ravine to the Sylvan
Booth honeymoon cottage, which has since been relocated.
Documents discovered in the Taliesan archives since publication of the first edition of this book indicate that the
cottage may have been authored by Wright.

Ravine Bluffs Development

188 Charles R. **Perry** Residence (1915)
Glencoe, Illinois

The Ravine Bluffs Development included five houses for rent. Each is here named for the first known independent owner. All are of plaster surface, with wood trim, and none were supervised by Wright. All may be variants of designs prepared for Edward C. Waller, Sr. (30, 31, 47, 65, 66), and Jr. (180), for Waller Estates in River Forest.

Ravine Bluffs Development

189 Hollis R. **Root** Residence (1915)
Glencoe, Illinois

This house appears to have survived with little need of
upkeep.

Ravine Bluffs Development
190 William F. **Kier** Residence (1915)
Glencoe, Illinois
An essentially square-plan house, the Kier residence is topped by a hipped roof.

Ravine Bluffs Development
191 William F. Ross Residence (1915)
Glencoe, Illinois
The porch (at left in the photograph) is not by Wright.

Ravine Bluffs Development
192 Lute F. **Kissam** Residence (1915)
Glencoe, Illinois

The original timbers show weakening in the open porch
extension of the main square of the house.

193 Emil **Bach** Residence (1915)
Chicago, Illinois

Here Wright employed cantilever design to allow the second story to overhang the first. The brick is unchanged, but wood and plaster are now painted.

194, 195 **Imperial Hotel** (1915) and **Annex** (1916)
Tokyo, Japan
Hotel demolished, 1968 (entrance lobby reconstructed at
Meiji Village near Nagoya, Japan, 1976)
Annex demolished, 1923

Wright's major work in Japan, the Imperial Hotel made
liberal use of soft lava, Oya stone. The hotel's floating foundation permitted it to survive, with little damage, the great
earthquake of September 1, 1923. It was employed, and
altered, by the American army following World War II.
Apparently Wright was offered the opportunity to remodel
the structure at this time but refused. As downtown-Tokyo
land values rose, it became more feasible to tear down the
building than to renovate it. Japan's tradition of beauty,
however, would not allow the building to vanish completely; the entrance lobby was dismantled and taken to Nagoya.
It was reconstructed on the western reaches of the Meiji-
mura open-air architectural museum and opened to the
public in March 1976. (Photograph of lobby reconstruction
by Masami Tanigawa.)

196 F. C. **Bogk** Residence (1916)
Milwaukee, Wisconsin

A post-Prairie house in Roman brick and of square plan, the Bogk residence facade is most strikingly ornamental.

197 Ernest **Vosburgh** Residence (1916)
Grand Beach, Michigan

Wright designed three houses in Grand Beach, and only the Vosburgh remains essentially as built. It is a Prairie gem of cruciform plan with a two-story-high living room, set near a creek that flows through the woods to nearby Lake Michigan.

198   Joseph J. Bagley Residence (1916)
Grand Beach, Michigan

Leaning over the precipice that leads down to Lake Michigan from a knoll considerably above street level, the Joseph Bagley summer home spreads into several one-story wings from its single two-story unit. It has been extensively remodeled, with much glass added and metal replacing wood trim.

199 W. S. Carr Residence (1916)
Grand Beach, Michigan

This cottage, now winterized, sits on the edge of the high
bluffs leading down to Lake Michigan. Originally of plaster
with wood trim, it has been added to, resurfaced, and extensively altered throughout.

200 Arthur **Munkwitz Duplex Apartments** (1916)
Milwaukee, Wisconsin
Demolished

As early as 1911 Wright was designing his American System Ready-Cut structures with pre-fabricated construction integral to their concept. In 1916, the idea was again taken up, resulting in these buildings for Arthur Munkwitz and his partner Arthur L. Richards (171, 201-203). They are based on the American Model A4 home. Each apartment features a living room the full width of the front facade. An adjoining dining space overlooks the entry, while the kitchen balances the plan. The stairwells and hall separate these spaces from the bathroom and pair of bedrooms in each unit, these latter defining the rear of the structure. Two of the Model A4 units, one above the other, form a duplex. Perhaps the joining of pairs of such duplex apartments at a common entryway justifies use of the term, "quadraplex" apartment.

201 Arthur L. **Richards Duplex Apartments** (1916)
Milwaukee, Wisconsin

These are four separate buildings, each with upper and
lower apartments. Originally all were of plaster surface with
wood trim; two have been resurfaced. All are from American System Ready-cut prefab plans of 1911, and all have
been somewhat altered. None were supervised by Wright
during construction.

202 Arthur L. **Richards Small House** (1916)
Milwaukee, Wisconsin

Just east of the Richards Apartments (201) lies this small, single-story flat-roofed house. It is from American System Ready-cut prefab plans.

203 Arthur L. **Richards Bungalow** (1916)
Milwaukee, Wisconsin

Next to the Richards Small House (202) is this bungalow,
now resurfaced with stone veneer. In its original form, it
looked much like the second Hunt residence (204). Both
are American System prefabs. Documentation is not yet
sufficient to determine whether or not similar units in
Wilmette and Lake Bluff, Illinois, are "pirated," or
deserving of inclusion in these listings.

204 Stephen M. B. **Hunt Residence II** (1917)
Oshkosh, Wisconsin

This building follows the same basic plan as the Richards
Bungalow (203).

205 Henry J. **Allen** Residence (1917)
Wichita, Kansas

In his fiftieth year of fruitful life, Wright began moving
west, pausing on his way for this, his first building and only
house in Kansas. Although on initial inspection the Allen
house looks like a brick Prairie type, it actually encloses a
garden court from the noise of passing autos. In this detail
it breaks with Prairie principles and tends toward Japanese
forms. The house and grounds were completely restored for
A. W. Kincade in 1971-1972.

206 Aisaku Hayashi Residence (1917)

Tokyo, Japan

Wright did not do complete plans for this structure but apparently made only sketches, the details being filled out by the craftsmen involved in its construction. Oya stone (soft lava block) is trimmed with wood. The living room, which is the part of this structure most characteristic of Wright's style, faces south over an open field to what is now the Komazawa Olympic Park. Hayashi was general manager of the Imperial Hotel (194). As of 1972 the building was owned by the Dentsu Advertising Company of Tokyo.

Arinobu **Fukuhara** Residence (1918)
Hakone, Japan
Demolished by earthquake, 1923

All that is known of this structure is the surname of the client and the general location of the house. It was destroyed by an earthquake.

208 Aline **Barnsdall Hollyhock House** (1917),
209 Little Dipper **Kindergarten** (1920),
210, 211 **Studio Residence A** (1920), and **B** (1921)
Los Angeles, California
Kindergarten and Studio Residence B demolished

Commanding the western view as the major structure in Barnsdall Park, Hollyhock House, so named for its ornamental forms, suggests a Mayan temple. Its exposed poured-concrete structure was built about 1920. Earliest sketches of this building as it appears in constructed form may be dated as early as 1913. Hollyhock House was given to the city of Los Angeles in 1927. The Olive Hill Foundation—Barnsdall Park of today was the former Olive Hill—reconstructed the building in 1947. Then it became part of the Los Angeles Municipal Art Museum and, after early 1970s reconstruction, is now open to the public. The only other part of the Wright-designed Barnsdall Park complex that remains today, the Studio Residence A, reveals some imprint of R. M. Schindler, who supervised its construction, then went on to fame of his own in southern California. It is now used as a classroom-studio space by the Los Angeles Parks and Recreation Department. Landscaping of Olive Hill was designed by Lloyd Wright, but it has been altered during various reconstructions and recent additions to the

grounds. Hollyhock House has been designated by the AIA as
one of seventeen American buildings designed by Wright to
be retained as an example of his architectural contribution
to American culture.

Barnsdall Studio Residence A

212 Tazaemon Yamamura Residence (1918)
Ashiya, Japan

This house is perched on a promontory above the left bank of the Ashiyagawa River, facing south to Osaka Bay. Four stories lift it up the hillside, and one 120-degree bend takes it around its eastern slope. Oya stone and Lauan (Philippine mahogany) are the prime construction materials. Owned in 1972 by the Yodogawa Seiko (Yodogawa Steel Company) of Osaka and used as a company dormitory, the structure was saved from a scheduled 1975 demolition.

213 Jiyu Gakuen Girls' School (1921)
Tokyo, Japan

This school is known to many in English as the "School of the Free Spirit." L-shaped, single-story wings jut out from the central, two-story rectangle of this Oya stone and wood structure. The living room is of two stories, with interior balcony. Construction was supervised by Arata Endo, a practitioner of organic architecture whose son is a former Taliesin Fellow and successful Japanese architect. These two architects are largely responsible for the new Jiyu Gakuen School in the countryside west of Tokyo. Wright's "old" Jiyu Gakuen School remains a school for girls, and permission may be obtained from the headmistress to visit its interior.

214 Mrs. George Madison **Millard** Residence,
"La Miniatura" (1923)
Pasadena, California

This is the first of four textile-block houses constructed in
the Los Angeles area. Its two-story high living room is deli-
cately lit by pierced, patterned block and overlooks a lovely
pool surrounded by lush gardens deep in the ravine-tra-
versed site (plan of main floor included towards the rear of
this book). The face relief patterns of the blocks vary for
each project. The method of construction consisted of
stacking concrete blocks three inches thick, cast in molds,
next to and atop one another without visible mortar joints.
In all but La Miniatura, thin concrete and steel reinforcing
rods were run horizontally and vertically in edge reveals
"knitting" the whole together. A double wythe was common, held together by steel cross ties, the cavity air space
serving as insulation. After World War II, this knitting
process, called "knit block" (and not to be confused with
W. B. Griffin's totally different "knitlock" system) gave rise
to the "Wright textile block." All four of the California
block houses (214-217) were supervised in construction by
Lloyd Wright, eldest son of the architect. He also provided
the landscaping and design of the 1926 studio addition.

215 John **Storer** Residence (1923)
Hollywood, California

This is the second of the four Los Angeles area textile-block houses. Its lowest story contains a variety of work spaces, but the second (public entrance) floor features a two-story-high living room, textile block throughout. One side opens from the hillside perch to a full view of Hollywood, Los Angeles, and the San Bernardino Valley. The other looks onto a courtyard, sunk into the rising hillside. The Storer house was supervised during construction by Lloyd Wright, who also designed the landscaping.

216 **Samuel Freeman** Residence (1923)
Los Angeles, California

Still owned and occupied by the client at this publication, this third of the California textile-block houses clings to the Hollywood foothills of the Santa Monica Mountains. Living room, kitchen, and garage are on the entry level, and sleeping quarters and terrace are one story below. Eucalyptus, common pine painted redwood red, and both plain and patterned textile block are the materials employed in construction. The project was supervised by Lloyd Wright, who also did the working drawings and landscaping; and one of the architect's students, R. M. Schindler, designed the Freeman's furniture.

217   Charles **Ennis** Residence (1923)
Los Angeles, California

The last of the four Los Angeles textile-block houses, the
Ennis is the most monumental. Anywhere along Vermont
Avenue, looking north, one sees it completing its ridge on
the southern reaches of the Santa Monica Mountains. Its
views are to both Griffith Park, on the north, and the Los
Angeles metropolitan area, on the south. The textile block
pattern is almost symmetrical about the diagonal of its
square surface. While in the Freeman house (216) blocks
are paired, one mirroring the other, here they usually are
given the same orientation, and in the Arizona Biltmore
Hotel and Cottages (221, 222) the pattern is complete only
when the blocks are paired. Lloyd Wright supervised construction, prepared the working drawings, and designed the
landscaping.

218, 219 Frank Lloyd Wright, **Taliesin III** (1925ff) and **Dams** (1945)
220 Mrs. Frank Lloyd Wright, **Enclosed Garden at Taliesin** (1959)
Spring Green, Wisconsin

"Taliesin" is the name of Wright's home in Wisconsin. It is from the Welsh for "the shining brow"; Taliesin does not sit on a hill but rather clings to its brow above the left bank of the Wisconsin River, looking north and east. Actually there have been three Taliesins, the first built in 1911 (172), the second in 1914 (182). There is also a Taliesin West (241), plus perhaps even a "Taliesin the Third" as the Hotel Plaza Apartment Remodeling (381) was known. The current Taliesin was rebuilt in 1925 after destruction by fire. As in 1914, only living quarters were destroyed, and much of Taliesins I and II remains in Taliesin III. Constructed mostly of native limestone, wood, and plaster surfacing, it has been continually altered in keeping with the needs of the Wrights and the Taliesin Fellowship. The dams in the valley have created a small lake that is used for recreation as well as to control water flow through the farm land. The garden design, Wright's last sketch, was built for Mrs. Wright in the summer of 1959. Taliesin is one of seventeen buildings by Wright that has been designated by the AIA to be retained as an example of his architectural contribution to American culture. (Upper photograph next page supplied by Bradley Ray Storrer, AIA.)

Taliesin III

221 Warren McArthur, **Arizona Biltmore Hotel**
222 and **Cottages** (1927)
Phoenix, Arizona

Both hotel and cottages are Wright's work. Though attributed by some to Albert McArthur, son of Warren McArthur (11-13), who had begun work in Wright's Oak Park studio in 1908, the younger McArthur's major activity in this project was preparation of the working drawings. The hotel is perhaps the largest textile-block design by Wright. The cottages come in both T and rectangular plans, single- and two-story. Entrance to the Biltmore grounds is at 24th Street and Missouri Avenue, and the hotel is open during the fall, winter, and spring.

Arizona Biltmore Cottages

223 **Beach Cottages, Dumyât, Egypt** (1927)
Demolished

These cottages were prefabricated structures designed to be disassembled each year and stored during the spring flood season.

224 Frank Lloyd Wright, **Ocatillo Desert Camp** (1928)
Chandler, Arizona
Demolished

Wright's association with Dr. Alexander Chandler was for the most part unfruitful. Projects never realised from this year and for this client alone included San Marcos-in-the-Desert (a resort hotel), San Marcos Hotel alterations, San Marcos Water Gardens, a simple block house, and a residence for Owen D. Young. The Ocatillo Desert Camp, constructed of wood and material much like the later Taliesin West (241), was a temporary residence for Wright during the period in which these designs for the Chandler, Arizona, area were in progress.

225 **Darwin D. Martin Residence, "Graycliff"** and
226 **"Graycliff" Garage** (1927)
Derby, New York

Graycliff was built as a summer home for Darwin D. Martin.
It sits a scant 25 yards from the gray cliff whose precipice
drops directly to Lake Erie. The residence structure, probably originally of plaster surfacing with wood trim and
stone fireplaces and chimneys, has been resurfaced. In the
early 1970s it was serving as a residence for the Piarist
Fathers. The garage may have been started in 1926. Wright
did not supervise the construction of either building.

Graycliff Garage

227 Richard Lloyd Jones Residence, "Westhope" (1929)
Tulsa, Oklahoma

Wright's first project in Oklahoma was for his cousin,
Richard Lloyd Jones, founder of the *Tulsa Tribune*. No
one view reveals the true dimension of this accomplishment
in glass and textile block. The dwelling, two stories high for
only a third of the plan, encloses a raised inner courtyard
with swimming pool. Built on a five-foot module, it employs
concrete blocks inside and out that are one-third by one-
fourth of the module in surface dimension. The structure
has been modified for modern conveniences such as air conditioning (with vents concealed behind the grillwork of the
cut-out Mayan-design blocks), and kitchen and master bedroom have been enlarged by combining earlier smaller
rooms. Three decorative extensions of the interior space
(one shown in the photograph) were originally aviaries but
now serve as miniature greenhouses.

228 Frank Lloyd Wright, **Taliesin Fellowship Complex** (1933ff)
Spring Green, Wisconsin

The Great Depression left Wright with few commissions,
but instead of retiring in 1932 at the age of sixty-five, he
entered a whole new era of creativity. He founded the
Taliesin Fellowship (two of the first apprentices were
William Wesley Peters, now a Frank Lloyd Wright Foundation vice-president, and John H. Howe), remodeled the
Hillside Home School II (69) including Hillside Playhouse
(burned, rebuilt in 1952) for use by the Fellowship, and
began work on his concept of a Broadacre City and then
the Usonian home. His scheme for a truly American city
was realized on a grand scale in models and in a few scat-
tered works—for example, the Affleck house (274), Suntop
Homes (248), and Lindholm Service Station (414)—but
never in the way Wright wanted, in a complete city or in a
new concept of American city planning universally applied.

229 Malcolm E. **Willey** Residence (1933)
Minneapolis, Minnesota

The Willey house, the latter of two designs by Wright for
the client, is of dark red sand and paving bricks, with cypress trim. It is a single-story structure located on a former
bluff above the Mississippi River, which was disfigured in
the 1960s by the intrusion of Interstate Highway 94. With
its central work space—Wright's term for a kitchen plus utilities core—directly adjoining the living-dining room (center
in the photograph), it represents the major bridge between
the Prairie style and the soon-to-appear Usonian house plan.
The radiator floor heating in this house is a direct forerun-
ner of the gravity heating characteristic of the Usonian
home. The elimination of servants' quarters is also typically
Usonian.

230 Edgar J. **Kaufmann**, Sr., **Residence "Fallingwater"** (1935),
31, 232 **Guesthouse** (1938), and **Guesthouse Alterations** (1948)
Ohiopyle, Pennsylvania

Aside from his own Taliesin Fellowship Complex, Wright
had seen only two of his projects constructed over a period
of almost eight years, from 1928 to 1935. Then, when the
architect was sixty-nine, came Fallingwater, the Johnson
Administration Building, and the Usonian home concept all
in one year, and Wingspread a year later. Fallingwater is perhaps the best-known private home for someone not of royal
blood in the history of the world. A main-floor plan is included following this catalog section. Perched over a waterfall deep in the Pennsylvania highlands, it seems part of the
rock formations to which it clings. Reinforced-concrete
cantilever slabs project from the rock band to carry the
house over the stream. From the square living room, one
can step directly down a suspended stairway to the stream.
Immediately above, on the third level, terraces open from
sleeping quarters, emphasizing the horizontal nature of the
structural forms; "the apotheosis of the horizontal" it has
been called and is one of seventeen buildings designed by
Wright that has been designated by the AIA to be retained
as an example of his architectural contribution to American
culture. Three years separated design of the main house and
the guesthouse. The Western Pennsylvania Conservancy
conducts guided tours during most of the year, except the
cold winter months; reservations are advised.

Kaufmann Guesthouse

233 Edgar J. **Kaufmann**, Sr., **Office** (1937)
Pittsburgh, Pennsylvania
Dismantled, stored, then reassembled in the Victoria and
Albert Museum, London

Wright's work for the downtown-Pittsburgh Kaufmann
Department Store included furniture and paneling. In *The
Natural House* Wright noted that sitting is "in itself an un-
fortunate necessity not quite elegant yet . . ." but admitted
that "it is possible now to design a chair in which any sitter
is compelled to look comfortable whether he is so or not."
Finally, "when the house-interior absorbs the chair as in
perfect harmony, then we will have achieved not so minor a
symptom of a culture of our own." To create this harmony
in the Kaufmann office, Wright's chairs and other furniture
are complemented by a cypress plywood mural in relief.

234 Herbert **Jacobs First Residence** (1936)
Westmoreland, now Madison, Wisconsin

This, the first-built Usonian house, promulgated concepts
already evolved in designs for H. C. Hoult and Robert D.
Lusk. Its structural characteristics include a concrete-slab
floor providing gravity heating, a masonry core and, for
most of the remainder, "dry wall" construction. As Wright
used the term, "dry wall" was not contemporary plaster-
board, but meant a sandwich type of assembly, a laminate
of three layers of wood boards screwed together. Eliminating conventional two-by-four studs, the center, insula-
ting, layer was often plywood. In this, the first of two
Wright-designed residences for Herbert Jacobs (the other,
283), brick was the masonry, and the dry wall used recessed
redwood battens, a reversal of Prairie board and batten
typical of Usonian practice. Spatially, the masonry core was
important. This "workspace"—kitchen, laundry, and such—
places the housewife at the heart of domestic activities.
Dining space was immediately adjacent for convenience.
Active space, the living room, extended in one direction,
quiet space, the bedrooms, in another. In the Jacobs first
residence, these spaces were joined by a 90 degree angle.
Future Usonian development would take this to 120 degree, 180 degree (in-line plan), and other angles, and
through more complicated modules, such as triangles and
parallelograms, than the simple two-by-four foot rectangle
and basic L plan employed here. Lastly, the gravity (radiant) heating is a development of the "Korean room" principle Wright first encountered on a damp winter's eve in the
Tokyo house of Baron Okura, the Emperor's Imperial Hotel
representative. Heat is drawn to a chimney through ducts in
floor tiles; Wright's adaptation for Usonian construction
involved slab floor-embedded pipes, carrying heated water,
to generate a spring-like environment.

235 Paul R. **Hanna** Residence, "Honeycomb House" (1936)
Stanford, California

Wright called this a wooden house. Though it uses common
wire-cut San Jose brick inside and out, many of the walls
are wood. The ease with which the nonmasonry walls could
be assembled or disassembled allowed for considerable alteration of interior space. This accommodated individual
bedrooms for children when the house was first built under
masterbuilder Harold Turner's supervision. These were later
converted to larger living spaces when the children left. All
changes were in accordance with Wright's original ideas. A
plan of the final version is at the rear of this book. The
Hanna house, maintained by Stanford University, is called
Honeycomb House because the Usonian structure's plan is
fashioned on a hexagonal unit system, a module that replaced the octagon as Wright's favorite from this time on.
The basic module unit is one foot one inch. Each redwood
board and recessed batten observes this spacing. Hexagons
marked in the slab floor have sides two units in length. One-
by-eight wall studs are on two-unit centers. Honeycomb
House completes the hillside to which it clings, its floor and
courtyard levels adjusting to the contours of the hill; it was
capped by a copper roof, now replaced with Heydite. It was
Wright's first work in the San Francisco region. This structure has been designated by the American Institute of Architects as one of seventeen American buildings designed by
Wright to be retained as an example of his architectural
contribution to American culture.

236 Mrs. **Abby Beecher Roberts** Residence, "Deertrack" (1936)
Marquette, Michigan

A few miles west of Marquette, a long hill slopes southeast-ward through evergreen forests. Commanding this view is Deertrack, home of Abby Beecher Roberts. This engaging lady once cast Wright's horoscope around the then-accepted 1869 birthdate. Finding it not to fit the man as she knew him, she discovered that the fit was perfect for 1867, his actual year of birth. Her home has been expanded.

237 **S. C. Johnson** and Son **Administration Building** (1936) and
238 **Research Tower** (1944) for H. F. Johnson, president,
Johnson Wax Company
Racine, Wisconsin

Both the Administration Building (also called the Johnson
Wax Building) and the later Research Tower (rising at left
in the photograph) are of brick and glass. The main office
work space is articulated by dendriform columns capable of
supporting six times the weight imposed upon them, a fact
Wright had to demonstrate in order to obtain a building
permit. The glass is not in panes, but in tubing, and several
layers of different sizes are used to admit light but no view.
Industrial air pollution caused the tubes in recent years to
collect dirt; new synthetic resins now permit a permanent
seal to be achieved. Wright designed all the original furniture
for the building, including the three-legged secretary chairs,
which tip over if one does not sit with correct posture. The
tower is totally enclosed and does not allow for horizontal
expansion of work space. Free tours are conducted during
regular business hours. Herbert F. Johnson, grandson of
S. C. Johnson, also commissioned Wingspread (239). Both
the Administration Building and the Tower have been designated by the American Institute of Architects as two of
seventeen American buildings designed by Wright to be
retained as examples of his architectural contribution to
American culture.

239 Herbert F. Johnson Residence, "Wingspread" (1937)
Wind Point, Wisconsin

Herbert F. Johnson commissioned the Johnson Wax Building (237) as well as Wingspread; the latter is now head-
quarters of The Johnson Foundation. Wingspread is the last
of the Prairie houses. Its pinwheel plan is zoned—that is,
sleeping quarters are in the wing shown below, kitchen in
the opposite, and so forth. This pinwheel, as Wright employs
it, a simple variant of his favorite cruciform plan, extends
from a central, three-story-high octagon. Pink Kasota sand-
side walls of the swimming pool, shown on next page, were
undercut so that they seem to disappear, leaving only water
and reflection. Wright considered this his most expensive
and best-built house to date, and he noted that many had
thought the site undistinguished until he placed the house
on it. West wing carports (not shown here) have been converted into office space. A plan of the structure as originally conceived by Wright is in the section following the
catalog part of this book. Supervision of the three projects
for Herbert F. Johnson, Wingspread and the Johnson Wax
complex, was by masterbuilder Ben Wiltscheck.

Herbert F. Johnson Residence and Swimming Pool

240 Ben **Rebhuhn** Residence (1937)
Great Neck Estates, New York

This house follows a cruciform plan and has a two-story-high living room. Cypress board and batten plus brick inside and out are the primary materials of construction. Stylistically, it appears to be a Usonian reworking of the Vosburgh house (197).

Taliesin West, Wright's winter home on Maricopa Mesa for the Taliesin Fellowship, offered a new challenge in materials. The architect's primary solution was what he called "desert rubblestone wall" construction. There are many ways of achieving this, but all involve randomly placing large stones into forms, then pouring concrete around the stones while leaving most of the face next to the form exposed. In the Bott house (404) wet sand was forced between form and stone surface before the concrete was poured. In the Austin house (345) crumpled newspaper, instead of sand, was used to keep the stone faces from being covered with concrete. At Taliesin West, the grouting was allowed to seep around the edges of the stone face, then surplus was chipped away to reveal the stone surface. Often, washing with acid was employed to bring out color in the stone.

In the dry heat of the Arizona desert, Wright found that stretched linen canvas provided an ideal shield against flash thunderstorms and the sun's glare. Fitted to redwood frames, the two materials adjusted most effectively, if sometimes noisily, to rapid and wide temperature changes. Fiberglass and steel now replace much of the original structure.

Taliesin West has been designated by the AIA as one of seventeen American buildings to be retained as an example of Wright's architectural contribution to American culture. It houses the Fellowship the greater part of the year, and Taliesin Fellows conduct tours throughout the day. (Photograph 242 by Bradley Ray Storrer, AIA.)

Taliesin West, detail

Taliesin West, Sign

246 Frank Lloyd Wright, **Midway Barns** (1938) with
247 Dairy and Machine Sheds (1947)
Spring Green, Wisconsin

Under Wright's guidance, every Taliesin Fellow started his apprenticeship by working in and with the earth. Under the care of the apprentices, the rich Wisconsin soil provided much fresh food to the dinner tables shared by the entire Taliesin community. The first barns, located midway between Hillside and Taliesin, and the later dairy and machine sheds served the needs of an expanding architectural community in midwestern Wisconsin.

248 Otto Mallery of Tod Company, **Suntop Homes** (1938)
Ardmore, Pennsylvania

Based upon a Broadacre City model, these units have been
known as Suntop Homes, Cloverleaf, Quadruple Housing,
and The Ardmore Experiment. The original Suntop Homes
project was for the United States Government on a tract
near Pittsfield, Massachusetts. A change in housing administration and complaints from local architects that they,
not an "outsider," should do the project prevented its construction. There were to have been four of these units in
Ardmore, built in a row but each angled differently on the
sites. Only one was built. The building is divided into quarters, each of two stories plus basement and sunroof, and
houses four families. The exterior is of brick and horizontal
lapped wood siding; this siding is imitated in the wall now
surrounding the structure. Construction was supervised by
masterbuilder Harold Turner, whose other efforts include
some of Wright's major statements: residences for Hanna,
Affleck, Armstrong, Christie, Goetsch-Winckler and Rebhuhn. Damage to two of the apartments has caused reconstruction that is not in accord with Wright's plans.

249 Charles L. **Manson** Residence (1938)
Wausau, Wisconsin

The Manson house was one of Wright's attempts to move away from the L-plan home by varying the angle at which the living room intersected the remainder of the house. The diagonal arrangement here achieved, both with living room at one end and master bedroom and carport at the other, found easier expression when Wright abandoned the rectangular modules (a four-foot square in Manson) to investigate triangles and parallelograms. A dropped ceiling is employed at the children's bedrooms, so that a second-story darkroom for the photographic couple could be accommodated within a height but a few feet greater than that for a single story structure. The house, mostly of brick, is sheathed and partitioned by regular board and batten walls.

250 Rose **Pauson** Residence (1939)
Phoenix, Arizona
Mostly demolished
Only ruins remain after a 1942 fire. The desert rubblestone
wall construction is fully revealed in the ruins, though the
horizontal character of the structure is largely lost in the
absence of the once-beautiful wood terraces and balconies.

Wright conceived the master plan for a whole college in 1938, although the realization of individual projects spanned the next decade and a half. Since Broadacre City never came to fruition, Florida Southern College offers the viewer a rare opportunity to see a unified plan of Wrightian thought on a city-planning scale. All the Florida Southern College structures employ textile block. Different plan modules are used; the Pfeiffer Chapel (251) is based on a diamond or double triangle, while the Roux Library (252)—not the new one on the northwest corner of the campus, but the one connected by Esplanades—is a large circle with diamonds. The areas between the three seminar buildings are now glassed in for additional office space. The Administration Building (255) is actually two structures with a garden courtyard between them. Esplanades link all of Wright's work on the Florida Southern College campus, and buildings not so linked are by other architects. Usually these esplanades stand free of other structures, but at the Science and Cosmography (256) and Industrial Arts (254) buildings they are an extension of the outer wall. The Minor Chapel (258) is so oriented on its site that the colored glass windows behind the altar are most effectively lit by the setting sun. Visitors to the campus are asked to report to the Administration Building before leaving their cars in campus parking lots.

Library

Pfeiffer Chapel

Industrial Arts Building

Administration Building

Science and Cosmography Building with Esplanades

259 Sidney **Bazett** Residence (1939)
Hillsborough, California

This second house by Wright in the San Francisco region clings to its hillside plot by angling around hexagonal modules into a Y plan. Brick and horizontal sunk redwood batten construction were used.

260 Andrew F. H. **Armstrong** Residence (1939)
Ogden Dunes, Indiana

Angles of 30, 60, and 90 degrees interlock rectangular
spaces in this house of brick and horizontal board and sunk
batten. The top level is sleeping quarters, with a third
bedroom added (on the right in the photograph), and the
upper story of the two-story-high living room. The middle
level is the living room and work space, and the lowest level
is carport and entry. The basic axis is north-south, with
two-story-high windows looking northeast from the living
room over the Indiana dunes. Alterations to enlarge living
room and work space, designed in 1964 by John H. Howe
along with the bedroom addition, have been in progress for
several years.

The residence, characteristic of all the structures of Auldbrass Plantation, features slanting exterior battered walls of clear native cypress lumber in natural finish. This was laid diagonally, approximately at 80 degrees to the horizon, in imitation of the live oak on the property, and held by brass screws. The module is the hexagon, though this idea is absent from the earliest constructed works on the plot, such as the manager's quarters, where walls are angled to each other at 120 degrees on square-module units. While the cottages and main house stand by themselves, the other structures were all interconnected by esplanades. The residence photograph emphasizes the esplanade that would have connected, along a swimming pool, to the two-story guesthouse. This latter was planned so as to receive its occupants either by land or by boat, on a canal cut from the nearby river channel. Auldbrass was intended to be a working plantation for owner Leigh Stevens, a specialist in time and motion studies who was always concerned with productivity. Fire totally destroyed the barn and chicken runs, and drippings from Spanish moss and live oak ate through the original copper roofing. Stanton and Jessica Stevens Loring are restoring the complex.

Stevens Residence

Stevens Cottages

Stevens Manager's Quarters

Stevens Stables with Kennels

Lloyd Lewis Residence (1939) and **Farm Unit** (1943)
Libertyville, Illinois

This cypress and brick structure's living room and balcony
are on the upper story above ground-level entrances and the
bedroom wing. The farm unit is a poultry shed. Both structures are surrounded by dense forest, with light admitted
across the Des Plaines River. Mr. Lewis was editor of the
Chicago Daily News.

267 Stanley **Rosenbaum** Residence (1939) and
267A **Addition** (1948)
Florence, Alabama

Wright's only work in Alabama is an L-plan Usonian house
enlarged to a T plan by Wright in 1948. It has been kept in
excellent condition and was completely renovated in 1970.
The addition created a Japanese garden outside the new
living and master bedroom quarters.

268 Loren **Pope** (Pope-Leighey) Residence (1939)
Falls Church, Virginia (relocated to Mount Vernon,
Virginia, in 1964)

Horizontal sunk cypress batten dry-wall construction
around a brick core identify this as a Usonian house. It was
moved in 1964 from Falls Church to its present site at
Woodlawn Plantation, where it is open to visitors during the
summer months. New gravity heat slab was laid, and the
original dry wall and masonry core set thereon. This, however, was oriented quite differently than at its first site. The
play of sunlight through clerestory and other piercings of
the siding and overhang, intended by Wright, was thus destroyed. Another aesthetic factor, altered to ill effect in the
shift from Falls Church to the present site, is the approach;
it is now downhill and the flat roof is exposed to view.
Ownership and further restoration efforts are now entrusted to the National Trust for Historic Preservation.

269 Goetsch-Winckler Residence (1939)
Okemos, Michigan

In this Usonian unit built for Alma Goetsch and Katherine
Winckler, brick finds its way beyond the core into the extremities. The dry wall is a typical Usonian horizontal sunk
redwood batten sandwich. The house was originally part of
a project for teachers at what is now Michigan State University; only one other unit from the master plan was built,
the Rubin house (343) in Canton, Ohio.

270 Joseph **Euchtman** Residence (1939)
Baltimore, Maryland

This Usonian house carefully shuts out of view its close neighbor to the north and takes maximum advantage of its wedge-shaped lot, which most architects would have shunned. Its view southwest and southeast is across broad boulevarded spaces, yet it offers occupants complete privacy.

271 Bernard **Schwartz** Residence (1939)
Two Rivers, Wisconsin

The September 26, 1938, issue of *Life* magazine published
Wright's idea for a house "For a Family of $5000-$6000
Income," and the following year it was built on the right
bank of East Twin River at Still Bend in Two Rivers, Wisconsin. The house is of brick and horizontal cypress board
and sunk batten. Its two stories suggest a designation never
accorded it by the architect himself, the "two-story Usonian"
structure. The plan is a T, on a three-foot six-inch module.
It is so angled on its plot as to gain a full view east and south
along East Twin River without obstruction from neighboring
buildings.

272 George D. **Sturges** Residence (1939)
Brentwood Heights, California

Most of this house is cantilevered out from its hillside perch.
The brick and painted wood siding (the original was stained)
present an appearance of a house without windows; actually
the entire east wall, including living room and bedrooms,
opens to a balcony (on the left in the photograph) overlooking the street below.

273 John C. **Pew** Residence (1939)
Shorewood Hills, Wisconsin
The hillside site slopes gently from Mendota Drive, then
drops sharply to Lake Mendota. With its base on the slope
and one wing over the precipice, this limestone and cypress
structure is able to open its first floor to lake and woods
and preserve privacy for its second-story sleeping quarters.

274 Gregor **Affleck** Residence (1940)
Bloomfield Hills, Michigan

Here the sun room and sleeping quarters rest on the ground
while the living-dining space is cantilevered with the balcony
a half-story lower. The cypress siding has weathered to a
nice gray. An L, or F, plan, the house is taken from the
Broadacre City model of a "home for sloping ground."
Wright designed a second home for Mr. Affleck, whom he
knew as a boy when both lived in Spring Green, which was
not built.

275, 276 Arch **Oboler Gatehouse** (1940), **Retreat** (1941), and
  275A,B **Additions** (1944, 1946)
Malibu, California
With additions designed in 1944 and 1946 by Wright, this
living complex is still "in construction." The main structure
was to be known as "Eaglefeather." Desert rubblestone wall
construction is used throughout, with horizontal wood siding. Situated high in the Santa Monica Mountains above
Malibu, the retreat commands a stunning view across mountain wilderness.

Arch Oboler Retreat

277 Theodore **Baird** Residence (1940)
Amherst, Massachusetts

Wright's only work in Massachusetts is a Usonian type of
brick and horizontal cypress board and sunk batten. The
plan is an I configuration, expanded at one end and at
the center for the living room (left and center in the
photograph).

278 James B. **Christie** Residence (1940)
Bernardsville, New Jersey

An L plan with living room dominating the end of one leg,
this project was not supervised in construction by Wright.
It is located in thick woods on gently sloping grounds.

279 Clarence **Sondern** (Sondern-Adler) Residence (1940)
Kansas City, Missouri

The original structure for Sondern was Usonian. Eight years later Wright added a large living room a quarter-story below the Usonian structure for Arnold Adler (307). The composite T plan encloses a terrace just above the steep drop to Roanoke Parkway. The residence is only a mile away from the Kansas City Community Christian Church (280).

280 Kansas City Community Christian Church (1940)
Kansas City, Missouri

This structure was not supervised by a Taliesin fellow.
Some argue that this explains its being highly altered from
Wright's original intent. But Ben Wiltscheck, masterbuilder
of Wingspread (239) and the Johnson Wax complex (237-
238) was its supervisor; whatever changes were made had
to pass his inspection, and on-site alterations were common
in Wright's work of this time. It is built on a parallelogram
module and is open daily to visitors.

281 Carlton David **Wall** Residence, "Snowflake" (1941)
Plymouth, Michigan

Employing hexagonal forms, this brick and cypress structure curls around its rolling hill site, creating an enclosed
patio. The living room opens to terrace space looking west
and north (shown in photograph). An aerial view reveals
the snowflake geometry of the central living space. Immediately adjacent is the Goddard house (364).

282 Stuart **Richardson** Residence (1941)
Glen Ridge, New Jersey

If the Richardson house used less brick and more wood, it would be easy to call it a Usonian type. It is most notable as an early example of Wright's use of triangular forms, in the plan of the living room, derived from a hexagonal concept. The plan is a built version of the Vigo Sundt project, which was the progenitor of a significant number of triangular plans.

283 Herbert **Jacobs Second Residence** (1943)
Middleton, Wisconsin

This is the second Wright house designed and built for the Jacobs family. It is the first solar hemicycle, of two stories, with its back set into the earth. Its glassed private facade opens onto a sunken terrace.

Lowell **Walter Residence** (1945) and **River Pavilion** (1948)
Quasqueton, Iowa

Half of the buildings from Wright's imagination that still
stand in 1973 were created by 1938, though half of his
thousand projects would not be on the drawing boards until the end of World War II. The war years halted most construction. Only three of Wright's 1941 designs were built,
and none from 1942. From his 1943 efforts only the Jacobs
second residence (283) saw relatively quick construction,
while the Guggenheim design (400) had to wait nearly a decade before the foundation was laid. In 1945 construction
activity resumed.

At Cedar Rock on the left bank of the Wapsipinicon River
is the Walter house and river pavilion. The pavilion is of
brick, but the main house derives from the "glass house"
for the *Ladies Home Journal*. It has a reinforced concrete
roof, with steel, glass, walnut, and brick elsewhere. Wright
called it his "Opus 497," and supervision during construction was by John deKoven Hill, one of the more notable
Taliesin Fellowship graduates.

Walter River Pavilion

286   Arnold Friedman Residence, "The Fir Tree" (1945)
Pecos, New Mexico

This is a summer house of desert rubblestone wall construction with roofing and siding of rough cedar shakes.

287 Melvyn Maxwell Smith Residence (1946)
Bloomfield Hills, Michigan
A Usonian structure of L plan, the Smith house was en-
larged by the Taliesin Associated Architects in 1969-1970.
Brick and cypress board and sunk batten are the basic ma-
terials used. Construction supervision was by John deKoven
Hill.

288 Douglas **Grant** Residence (1946)
Cedar Rapids, Iowa

This rectangular, three-story house is of limestone (quarried by the Grants from the surrounding property), steel, concrete roofs and floors, and a copper fascia. The reinforced-concrete roof is 127 feet long; the roof forms were supported by 150 poplar trees. Excavation began in September 1949, and the house was occupied fifteen months later. Entry to the structure, of four-foot module design, is at the top floor (on the left in the photograph), from which one descends to the living room (at right).

289 Alvin **Miller** Residence (1946)
Charles City, Iowa

This single-story, clerestory lighted stone and cypress house extends in its terraces and outdoor fireplace to the right bank of the Red Cedar River.

290 Chauncey **Griggs** Residence (1946)
Tacoma, Washington

Located at the foot of a hill on Chambers Creek, this house
features a two-story facade on the inside of its L plan. Soar-
ing postwar construction costs caused delays in construction. The concrete-slab floor was laid long before the concrete-block core was raised, a good stone being unavailable.
Siding and roofing are of cedar planks, arranged diagonally
on most surfaces, though horizontally on some. Logs had
originally been considered, and this finished product retains
the rustic simplicity of a log cabin, without sacrificing the
amenities that usually disappear in such a structure. Construction was supervised by Alan Liddle, a Washington
architect.

291 Unitarian Church (1947)
Shorewood Hills, Wisconsin

The rising, green copper roof of this edifice symbolizes hands held together in prayer. Limestone and oak are the prime construction materials; the limestone was hauled some thirty miles to the site by congregation members. The auditorium holds 250 people, or 400 if the adjacent hearth room is added. An additional wing, not visible in the photograph, is by the Taliesin Associated Architects. The building is open daily. This structure has been designated by the American Institute of Architects as one of seventeen American buildings designed by Frank Lloyd Wright to be retained as an example of his architectural contribution to American culture.

292 A. H. **Bulbulian** Residence (1947)
Rochester, Minnesota
One simple 120-degree angle serves both to fit this cement
brick and cypress structure to the brow of the hill and to
orient it to take fullest advantage of the morning sun at the
breakfast table and afternoon sun in the living room. It is a
very short distance from the Keys residence (321). (Photograph courtesy of Dr. A. H. Bulbulian.)

293 Amy **Alpaugh** Residence (1947)
Northport, Michigan

Brick, oak, and ash are the prime materials of this residence. The living room (at left in the photograph) turns southwest toward Lake Michigan and the den east to Grand Traverse Bay. The original T plan has been altered by addition of a greenhouse designed by Glen T. Arai Associates.

294 David I. **Weisblat** Residence (1948)
Galesburg, Michigan

The Galesburg Country Homes subdivision plan was drawn up in 1947. Three structures employ Wright textile block and wood. The method of construction dates to the four California block houses (214-217). The Weisblat house was the first of four structures that were eventually built. Its living room roof is cantilevered from the fireplace masonry core, so that the windows, comprising fully half the room's wall space, carry no load and need no intermediary supports. John H. Howe of the Taliesin Associated Architects was responsible for an addition to the basic T plan angled at 120 degrees (not shown in the photograph), dated 1960. Howe also supervised construction of all four Galesburg Country Homes.

Galesburg Country Homes

295 Eric **Pratt** Residence (1948)
Galesburg, Michigan

A long I plan with central living room, this house faces
southwest down a long, slow slope. The westernmost unit
of the Galesburg Country Homes, it is primarily of Wright
textile-block construction.

Galesburg Country Homes
296 Samuel **Eppstein** Residence (1948)
Galesburg, Michigan

This structure in the Galesburg Country Homes master plan
is another I plan, oriented southwest-northeast with living
room at the northern extremity and garage beneath (in the
background of the photograph). In this particular unit, pre-
cision of the block construction is notable.

Galesburg Country Homes

297 Curtis **Meyer** Residence (1948)
Galesburg, Michigan

A solar hemicycle facing east down a gentle slope, the
Meyer house uses circles and circular segments throughout.
The central two-story drum sits in the crest of the hill,
enclosing stairs between the lower-floor living room and
the upper-level carport and bedrooms. The bedrooms look
over an inside balcony to the living room below (right in
the photograph), giving that room a two-story-high ceiling.
Concrete block is the main construction material.

298-301 Parkwyn Village

298 Robert **Levin** Residence (1948)
Kalamazoo, Michigan

Parkwyn Village is near the western edge of Kalamazoo, on a bluff over a small lake. Several houses were designed in the master plan; only four were built. The Levin house has an interesting treatment of its living room facade; the windows are stepped out in several bays, a design feature continued in a trellis (visible in the photograph). This room faces southwest. Wright textile block and cypress are the materials employed. A wing (not visible in the photograph) was added in 1960 by John H. Howe of the Taliesin Associated Architects. Howe also supervised construction of all the Wright-designed houses in Parkwyn Village.

Parkwyn Village
299 Ward **McCartney** Residence and
299A,B,C **Additions** (1949)
Kalamazoo, Michigan

This Parkwyn Village house was built, with expansion expected, on a diamond (double equilateral triangule) module. Kitchen core and dining-living room area (on the right in the photograph) were built first, and the bedroom wing (on left) was added after only four months. Enclosure of the portal to the north and a carport came later, but all were designed by Wright as part of the original plan and done in Wright textile block and mahogany. This, and the Anthony house (315), develop the triangle module idea first expressed in a cottage for Wright's sister, Maginel Wright Barney. A plan, without the final alterations, is included at the back of this book.

Parkwyn Village
300 Eric V. Brown Residence (1949)
Kalamazoo, Michigan

Mahogany is employed with Wright textile block in the Eric
Brown house, whose uphill roofline is at ground level. The
living room and attached terrace (at left in the photograph)
look out over broad fields to the pond below Taliesin Drive.

Parkwyn Village
301 Robert D. **Winn** Residence (1950)
Kalamazoo, Michigan

The Winn residence, situated at the dead end of Taliesin
Drive, is the only two-story unit of Wright's design in
Parkwyn Village. Its rectangular living room looks through
the hemicircular, enclosed, skylighted balcony. Wright textile block and wood are used. To the immediate north is a
house with a Wright-designed block, but that structure was
not built to Wright's plan.

302   Herman T. **Mossberg** Residence (1948)
South Bend, Indiana

This is a two-story L plan in red brick and cypress with
cedar shingles. The L encloses the patio on this corner lot.
The living room is the largest segment of the plan (foreground in the photograph), while the L wing contains sleeping quarters on the second floor, above kitchen and work
space. Construction was supervised by John H. Howe.
(Photograph courtesy of Denis C. Schmiedeke.)

303 J. Willis **Hughes** Residence, "Fountainhead" (1948)
Jackson, Mississippi

This is the only example of modern Wright architecture in
Mississippi, and a complete demonstration of organic principles in design. Concrete walls and slab floor, horizontal
board and batten interior paneling, and copper roof sit well
below street level. The bedroom wing terminates in a fountain over a pool that carries the 120-degree angle employed
in its plan out into the glen of this wooded site. A Fountainhead foundation is undertaking the full restoration of
the Hughes Residence.

304 Carroll **Alsop** Residence (1948)
Oskaloosa, Iowa

Only in the carport is the T plan suggested; interior space
seems to articulate an L. Brick is combined with cypress
and red asbestos-shingled roof. The plan is oriented to the
northeast, but the living room (on the right in the photograph) opens not only in that direction but also southeast.

305 Jack **Lamberson** Residence (1948)
Oskaloosa, Iowa

Perched on a gentle hilltop, this brick and cypress home
places equilateral triangles on a four-foot-square module. It,
and the Alsop residence (304) a short distance away,
apparently created a local revolution. Nine thousand
visitors saw these two houses when first constructed, in
1951. Supervision of construction was by Taliesin fellow
John deKoven Hill.

306 Mrs. Clinton **Walker** Residence (1948)
Carmel, California

This stone structure, built on the beach side of Scenic Road on Monterey Bay, lies mostly below street level, seemingly a natural extension of the rocky promontory at this curve in the beach front. Two materials have graced the living room roof, porcelain enamel, and copper. It is necessarily cantilevered from the masonry core so that no weight rests on the corbelling bands of glass. These windows block a direct breeze, but admit a gentle current of air. The master bedroom has been enlarged.

307 Arnold **Adler Addition** to **Sondern** Residence (1948)
Kansas City, Missouri

Wright's contribution here was a new living room, a quarter-story below the original early Usonian style structure. It appears in the foreground of the photograph.

308 Albert Adelman Residence (1948)
Fox Point, Wisconsin

In 1946 Wright designed a laundry building for Benjamin
Adelman and Son to be erected in nearby Milwaukee.
Though this was never built, two residences were constructed for the Adelman family—this structure, whose
covered walkway and garage turn the I plan into an L, and
a residence in Arizona (344). The living room separates
sleeping quarters at one end (right in the photograph) and
kitchen-dining area at the other. The house is oriented to
face south-southeast, and its western extremities are protected by shade trees. It is of buff-colored (integral color)
block, stepped out 3/4 inch every second course, cypress,
and cedar shakes.

309 Maynard P. **Buehler** Residence (1948)
Orinda, California

The living room of this concrete-block and wood house
(shown in the photograph) is offset to the L plan at 120
degrees so as to face west. Angling of the planes of the glass
facade under the broad rising eaves opens the view north
to nature and south to the swimming pool. The long leg of
the L includes sleeping quarters, and the short, work space.
The bedrooms open out to the swimming pool. Other structures on the grounds employ board and sunk batten to
blend with the one Wright-designed structure.

310 V. C. **Morris Gift Shop** (1948)
San Francisco, California

Originally a gift shop, the Morris shop has been renovated. It has since been used as an art gallery and dress shop. It is open during regular business hours. Its brick facade both protects internal contents and invites visitors to enter the portal. Circular forms are employed inside. This structure has been designated by the American Institute of Architects as one of seventeen American buildings designed by Wright to be retained as an example of his architectural contribution to American culture.

311 Charles E. **Weltzheimer** Residence (1948)
Oberlin, Ohio

This house is an L-plan structure of the Usonian type with, however, more masonry than was common. Clerestory detailing and fascia ornamentation is unique among Usonian projects. The first designs were for typically angular clerestory detail; later, three circles on a "branch," imitating perhaps the apple orchard on the property, appeared. The final design is more abstract. Many changes executed during construction do not show on Wright's plan, extensions and relocations of walls and entries near the storage space in particular. Restoration of other alterations since construction is by Ellen Johnson.

312 Erling P. **Brauner** Residence (1948)
Okemos, Michigan

The Brauner house was an attempt to redefine the Usonian house concept. Here, Wright textile block replaces brick and dry-wall construction. It is located across Arrow Head Road from the Edwards house (313) and only a short distance from the Goetsch-Winkler (269) and Schaberg (328) houses.

313 James **Edwards** Residence (1949)
Okemos, Michigan

A red brick and red Tidewater cypress house with red asphalt shingles and floors of red concrete containing radiant heating, the Edwards dwelling is built into a hillside with its rectangular spaces joined at 120-degree angles and a terrace the full length of the plan. The wing on the right in the photograph is a later addition made by the Taliesin Associated Architects in 1968. Refinishing of the exterior woodwork is a 1972 project of William T. Martin.

314 Henry J. **Neils** Residence (1949)
Minneapolis, Minnesota

Aluminum window framing—unusual for Wright— scrap
marble, cypress, and cedar shingles are combined in this
house on the east shore of Cedar Lake. It was designed on
a three-foot six-inch module and completed in April 1951.

315 Howard **Anthony** Residence (1949)
Benton Harbor, Michigan

Employing a diamond-shaped module, this dwelling sits
high above the right bank of the Saint Joseph River. Stone
is complemented by cypress and a roof of cedar shingles.

316 Sol Friedman Residence (1948)
Pleasantville, New York

Three Wright-designed homes were built close to each other
in this densely wooded, hilly countryside within commuting
distance north of New York City. The Sol Friedman house
on "Toyhill" was, in geometry, the most daring. It is a two-
story stone and concrete structure, interlocking two cylin-
ders, with a mushroom-shaped carport.

Usonia Homes
317 Edward **Serlin** Residence (1949)
Pleasantville, New York

The Serlin house, second of the Pleasantville projects, employs stone, as do its Usonian neighbors, but also uses some horizontal siding. Projected extensions at both east and west ends to complete Wright's design were never constructed.

Usonia Homes

318 Roland **Reisley** Residence (1951)
Pleasantville, New York

This last of the Pleasantville projects continues the use of
stone as the basic building material, with wood siding. It
wraps around the hillside with a 120-degree angle. It is a single-story structure, except in its masonry core, which also
has a balcony.

319 Kenneth **Laurent** Residence (1949)
Rockford, Illinois

The living room space of the Laurent residence (shown in
the photograph) opens northwest down a long slope leading
to the left bank of Spring Creek. Circular segments dominate the plan, interlocking with rectangular space in this
single-story solar hemicycle. Common brick complements
cypress. The house is so organized as to present no obsta-
cles to a wheelchair user; its plan is in a section at the back
of this book. Additions to the structure were the work of
John H. Howe.

320 Wilbur C. **Pearce** Residence (1950)
Bradbury, California

Though in plan the Pearce house superficially resembles the Laurent, site and materials dictated a different architectural expression. The Pearce house commands a location on a foothill of the San Gabriel Mountains in the Bradbury Hills. Its living room opens south to the San Gabriel Valley and north to the mountains and the Mount Wilson Observatory. The circular segments were constructed with concrete block. Roof and carport are cantilevered with steel. Concrete-slab floor with radiant heating, Honduras mahogany, and glass complete the list of construction materials. (Photograph courtesy of Mr. Pearce.)

321 Thomas E. **Keys** Residence (1950)
Rochester, Minnesota

Nineteen-fifty was a banner year for designing; twenty-one
projects were finally constructed. Nine were solutions of
use of concrete block, although the Keys residence was first
intended for stone. The house is trimmed with pine. It is
based on the berm-type housing for Detroit auto workers
of 1942, first shown as a $4000 project in the 1938 *Archi-
tectural Forum*. Additions made in 1971 by John H. Howe
enlarge the living room and convert the former carport to
a guestroom and bath.

322 David Wright Residence (1950)
Phoenix, Arizona

David Wright, the fourth child by the first Mrs. Frank Lloyd Wright, was involved in concrete block, its design, manufacture, and promotion. Consequently, when the designs David received from his father for a desert home were not of a construction system consistent with this concern, William Wesley Peters took on the re-engineering of the project for construction in block. The living spaces are all raised above ground and reached by a spiral rampway. This gives a curved in-line plan, with spaces no longer limited by orthogonal geometry. The heavily reinforced concrete floor, cantilevered from concrete block piers, carries air-conditioning ducts and other appurtenances. The block also features a decorative frieze echoing the plan's circular forms. Built-in furniture and the curving panels of the ceilings are of red Philippine mahogany. The roofing is metal, covered with a copper paint. From the living room, one may look over the almond-shaped pool past the entry ramp and across a carpet of green citrus orchard foliage to the rising sun or nearby mountains. Concealed lighting, some from outside the house, allows daytime furniture placement to serve after sunset. A guesthouse to the north is by John H. Howe. To the south is a home for David's son, David Lloyd Wright, designed by elder brother Lloyd Wright.

324 Richard **Davis** Residence, "Woodside" (1950)
Marion, Indiana

This painted concrete-block, cedar-shingled, and redwood-trimmed home derives from the Lake Tahoe project of 1922, a plan of several cottages and barges based on the concept of the Indian teepee. The living room rises the full height of the central "teepee," from which the 120-degree-angled wings extend.

325 J. A. **Sweeton** Residence (1950)
Cherry Hill, New Jersey

In the Sweeton dwelling a red concrete-slab floor with radiant heat is complemented by interior redwood plywood board and batten and a red roof. This roof, now covered with asbestos shingle, was originally laid out in board, overlapping so that two-foot strips ran the length of the structure, emphasizing the horizontal character of the design. Similar emphasis is given in the block, vertical grouting filling the joints to the block surface, horizontal grouting normally recessed. Both carport and fireplace are cantilevered. The module is a four-foot square, the plan a stubby T with an extension off the master bedroom (not visible in the photograph) for additional work space. Mrs. Sweeton designed and wove the original fabric for drapes and furniture.

326 Raymond **Carlson** Residence (1950)
Phoenix, Arizona

This house for the editor of *Arizona Highways* magazine is
of post and panel construction, using wood posts and insu-
lated cement asbestos panels. Angled southwest to northeast on its corner lot, it rises three stories. A prominent
clerestory takes advantage of light from the hot desert sun.
Landscaping now totally obscures the house from neighbors
and passers-by. (This photograph was taken in the early
1950s by Bradley Ray Storrer.)

327 John O. Carr Residence (1950)
Glenview, Illinois

This house is located on level ground deep into wooded country. Its roof along the entry sidewalk carefully steps around a great oak whose branches shelter the entire structure. It is a T plan in salmon-colored concrete block. The living room roof, an asymmetrical gable, is angled southwest to northeast to admit delightfully changing patterns of light both morning and evening. Patterned concrete block is used at the west end of the living room to divide living from kitchen areas; it rises to about eye level, but not to the ceiling, enhancing the sense of interior spaciousness.

328 Donald **Schaberg** Residence (1950)
Okemos, Michigan

Mr. Schaberg notes that his house was built with over
55,000 bricks inside and out. It is roofed with cedar shakes.
The original plan was an L; the bedroom wing (left in the
photograph) is southwest of the central kitchen and dining
section, and the northeast living room adjoins a carport that
juts northwest from the main entrance. An addition made
in the 1960s by John H. Howe, who supervised the original
construction, altered the plan to a U. With its own entrance
hallway leading from the main entryway down the northern
wall, the addition runs northwest from the bedroom wing.
The main view is over a broad, wooded valley.

329 Ina Moriss **Harper** Residence (1950)
Saint Joseph, Michigan

The living room of this L plan (at right in the photograph) turns from the bedroom axis to gain a view of Lake Michigan, directly across Lake Shore Drive. Salmon-colored (sand-mold) brick and cypress are employed throughout.

330 Robert **Berger** Residence (1950)
San Anselmo, California

Approaching from below, one could easily drive by this
house without seeing it, so deftly does it rest on one level
ridge of the steep slopes of these north bay hillsides. It is
best viewed overall from the opposite side of the valley,
but then one has to search to separate mountain from
desert rubblestone wall and wood, constructed on a triangular module.

331 Arthur C. **Mathews** Residence (1950)
Atherton, California

Two wings, parallel to each other, originate from the central workspace-plus-dining-area segment of this brick house.
To suit the diamond (double equilateral triangle) module,
the living room is at 120 degrees to the workspace, the
sleeping quarters at 60 degrees. Similarity of this plan to
that of the Richard Smith home (337) should be noted.

332 William **Palmer** Residence (1950)
Ann Arbor, Michigan

Constructed of cypress, sand-mold brick, and a matching
block fired the same as the brick, this house grows out of
the crest of a hill, opening from its triangular plan to a
curving plateau that welcomes the morning sun.

333 Isadore J. **Zimmerman** Residence (1950)
Manchester, New Hampshire

A long house with a clerestory lighting the central living
quarters, its primary construction material is brick. The true
spaciousness of this home is not apparent from the public
approach. Its view is to the southwest over a large, beauti-
fully landscaped yard.

334 Robert **Muirhead** Residence (1950)
Plato Center, Illinois

Common brick and cypress are the structural ingredients
of this very elongated plan on a four-foot module that runs
southwest to northeast over flat farmland. In the photograph the bedroom wing is to the left, living room in the
center, and utility space to the right.

335 Karl A. **Staley** Residence (1950)
North Madison, Ohio

This long I plan parallels the nearby Lake Erie shore, southwest to northeast, opening the living room to a northwest exposure. Aside from this one seemingly all-glass facade, the structure is of stone.

336 S. P. **Elam** Residence (1950)
Austin, Minnesota

A two-story stone and cypress structure, this house inter-locks triangles with rectangles. A rear terrace and the garage are additions not of Wright design.

337 Richard Smith Residence (1950)
Jefferson, Wisconsin

This house opens onto a yard just off the Meadow Springs
Golf Club. Limestone, plaster, cypress, and cedar shingles
are integrated in this structure.

338 John A. **Gillin** Residence (1950)
Dallas, Texas

One of Wright's most extensive single-story structures, the
Gillen house looks eastward over gently rolling lawns
through floor-to-ceiling glass. Living and dining spaces are
articulated more by the ceiling than by walls, as right angles
are avoided, even in the kitchenette facilities of the guest
rooms. Stone is the primary construction material, and
glass, rather than wood, might be called the secondary.
There are also plaster ceilings and soffits and a copper roof.

339 Seamour **Shavin** Residence (1950)
Chattanooga, Tennessee

Wright's only work in Tennessee is also one of the few of
the master's compositions that sit on, rather than wrap
around or fit into, the crest of the hill. The resulting view
of the Tennessee River and surrounding mountains is admitted to the house along its entire northern exposure.
This is heightened in the living room by the northward incline of the ceiling, drawing one's attention to the exterior
view. Native Tennessee limestone is the prime construction
material.

340 Russell W. M. **Kraus** Residence (1951)
Kirkwood, Missouri

This artist's house bends around the hill in which it nestles,
using triangular modules. The terrace door windows, designed by Mr. Kraus, are of geometrically patterned stained
glass in very delicate tints, mostly of blue and green. The
hilltop is open, while the downhill view is into wooded land.

341 Charles F. **Glore** Residence (1951)
Lake Forest, Illinois

This brick, cypress, and salmon concrete block two-story structure overlooks a ravine, guardian of the dwelling's privacy to the south. It is an in-line plan, with a children's room opening over the two-story living room; the flues of the fireplaces in both upper and lower rooms share the same masonry core. Other fireplaces warm the opposite end of the dwelling. After falling into severe disrepair, the building was renovated about 1973.

342 Patrick Kinney Residence (1951)
Lancaster, Wisconsin

Stone and wood are set on triangular modules, with living
room (at left in photograph) facing north and west. Former
Taliesin Fellow John Howe added a northeast wing, which
is detached from the main structure, in 1964.

343 Nathan **Rubin** Residence (1951)
Canton, Ohio

This house is essentially a mirror image of the Panshin
house, designed for the Usonian homes group in Okemos,
Michigan (269) but never built there. Brick and horizontal
wood siding sheathe the building whose sleeping quarters
and carport wing form a 120-degree angle.

344 Benjamin Adelman Residence (1951)
Phoenix, Arizona

A Usonian automatic house, the Benjamin Adelman residence has a two-story living room and kitchen lighted by the glass openings in the block pattern. Although its concept date is earlier than that of the Pieper residence (349), it was built after that house. The living room wall mural, with gilt and silvered mirror pieces, is by Eugene Masselink, who did many such designs for the Taliesin Fellowship.

345 Gabrielle and Charlcey **Austin** Residence,
"Broad Margin" (1951)
Greenville, South Carolina

Desert rubblestone wall construction was used in this house,
the exposed stone surfaces having been covered with newspaper before the cement was poured. This is one of the few
Wright houses where the sheltering roof is the characteristic
first noticed upon approach; it seems to extend the hill out
over the house. The entry hall, nestled in the hillside, serves
as a spine to the play, living, culinary, and sleeping quarters,
which all extend downhill off of this hall.

346 A. K. **Chahroudi** Residence (1951)
Lake Mahopac, New York

Located on the western shore of Klein's Island—historically,
Petra Island—in Lake Mahopac, this cottage is sheltered by
dense foliage. Desert rubblestone wall construction, some
horizontal wood sheathing, and triangular modules are combined in this residence.

347 Welbie L. Fuller Residence (1951)
Pass Christian, Mississippi
Demolished by Hurricane Camille, 1969

This house was in many ways unique among Wright's late
works. The structure was exposed natural concrete block
and rough-sawn yellow pine, post and beam, stained red.
Walls and ceilings were exposed natural asbestos board
sandwich panel with celotex core, placed between structural members; the similarity may be to the Carlson house
(326). The first floor was red concrete slab scored with a
fifty-two-inch module, main and third floors heart Southern yellow pine. Plate glass, bronze hardware, and gravel
surfaced flat roof with copper flashing complete the list of
materials of this house, which fell to the tidal wave of
Camille. The main living space was raised fully above
ground level. The entry, workspace, living room, and other
spaces opened to balconies and a terrace that extended to
an attached guesthouse. A third level contained bedrooms
and bath. Furnishings were all Wright designs.

Wright designed a complete service station and auto showroom for Wetmore, but they were never built. Later he designed the remodeling of the existing Wetmore facilities.
Though some remodeling was done, work never advanced
beyond the initial stages. Some evidence of this work—
wood trim—remains today.

The Pieper house is possibly the first constructed example
of a Usonian automatic house. In building the house,
Taliesin West student Pieper made the molds for the three-
inch-thick blocks, poured the concrete, knit the blocks
together with reinforcing steel rods and grouting, and eventually raised the entire structure, with some help from
Taliesin Fellow Charles Montooth. This is the "automatic"
aspect of construction; the client can make the project a
do-it-yourself home kit. Though two three-inch-thick walls
were considered, as in earlier Wright textile block designs
(214-217), and alternately a Usonian type sandwich insu-
lating interior wall, only one thickness of block was completed. Usonian automatic structures tend toward one thick
block wall, rather than two thin walls, for economy of construction, but the principle remains that of textile-block
building. The original plan was altered by addition of a
dining room by Arthur Lawton.

350 Ray **Brandes** Residence (1952)
Issaquah, Washington

Mr. Brandes was the builder of another, later Wright-designed house in the Seattle area (389). He notes the similarity of his own residence to the Goetsch-Winkler house (269). Although it may be similar in its central living room space, its site placement commands a more favorable relationship to the sun for this northwestern climate. The concrete-block retaining wall is not by Wright.

351 Quintin **Blair** Residence (1952)
Cody, Wyoming
The only work of Wright's design in Wyoming is this stone
and wood house on the plains east of Yellowstone National
Park. The rising living room ceiling opens to a view of the
entire eastern horizon. The southern porch has been enclosed.

352 Archie Boyd **Teater** Studio Residence (1952)
Bliss, Idaho

High on the bluffs above the right bank of the Snake River sits this, the only work by Wright in Idaho. Essentially a version of the "one-room house" generated from a 52-inch-wide parallelogram module, it features an immense studio room whose roof covers three-quarters of the house space with no interfering wall. Quartzite stone, concrete slab floor, and oak enclose the space. Plate glass, the highest nineteen feet above the foundation, opens the studio to a painter's northern light, instead of the southern exposure Wright would have otherwise provided. The knee-brace to the terrace roof is a later addition, not by Wright.

353 R. W. **Lindholm Residence**, "Mäntylä" (1952)
Cloquet, Minnesota

Mäntylä is a T plan so situated as to open living and sleeping quarters to the setting sun. Painted cement block is trimmed with wood. The Lindholms also built the Broadacre City Service Station in downtown Cloquet (414).

354 Frank S. **Sander** Residence, "Springbough" (1952)
Stamford, Connecticut

Springbough juts out from a rocky promontory toward the heavily wooded surroundings. Its well-shaded living room and balcony extension face south. Horizontal wood siding, now painted, complements brick foundation and core.

355 Harold Price, Sr., **Price Company Tower** (1952)
Bartlesville, Oklahoma

Based on the 1929 Saint Marks Tower project for William
Norman Guthrie, the Price Tower stands like a tall tree in
the rolling hills of eastern Oklahoma. The building is constructed of reinforced concrete with cantilevered floors,
copper louvers and copper-faced parapets, and gold-tinted
glass exterior. It is planned around a 60-degree parallelogram module 2' 6'' across, 1' 10 5/8'' on a side. Its nineteen
floors plus spire tower 221 feet above the prairie base. The
tower is open to visitors during regular business hours. This
structure has been designated by the American Institute of
Architects as one of seventeen American buildings designed
by Frank Lloyd Wright to be retained as an example of his
architectural contribution to American culture.

356 Anderton Court Shops (1952)
Beverly Hills, California

This group of shops in one building is located in the fashionable downtown section of Beverly Hills. Entrance to all shops is off a ramp that winds its way upwards, in parallelograms, around a central open wall. Wright showed a clear facade in his plans and was never offered the signs for approval.

357 Luis **Marden** Residence (1952)
McLean, Virginia

This is a hemicycle of block and wood. (Drawing delineated
by Harvey Ferrero.)

358 Robert **Llewellyn Wright** Residence (1953)
Bethesda, Maryland

A two-story hemicycle for Wright's sixth child by his first
wife, this concrete-block structure is wood faced at the
second story, where a balcony continues the hemicircular
line. Lloyd Wright landscaped the grounds in 1960.

359 George Lewis Residence (1952)
Tallahassee, Florida

The lower story of this two-story hemicycle is of concrete block, the upper, wood sheathed. The living room rises two stories.

360 Andrew B. **Cooke** Residence (1953)
Virginia Beach, Virginia

The points from which the concentric circles of the inner
and outer walls of the main living area were drawn are evident in the wedge segments of the patio floor. The brick is
baked from a clay imported from West Virginia, whose
color blends with the sand of Crystal Lake, next to which
the house stands. It is capped by a copper roof.

361 Jorgine **Boomer** Residence (1953)
Phoenix, Arizona

This house for a single person, which Wright designated a "mountain cottage," is compacted into two stories around a central chimney flue. It is of desert rubblestone wall construction with some horizontal wood sheathing, notably in the bedroom balcony. It looks north, away from the desert sun.

362 John J. **Dobkins** Residence (1953)
Canton, Ohio
Here the dominant feature is the living room with its glass
facade, which denies the rectangle in plan and in surface.
It receives sunlight from sunrise to sunset. Brick and wood
trim are combined with a copper roof. The residence is
located near the Feiman (371) and Rubin (343) houses.

363 Harold Price, Jr., Residence, "Hillside" (1953)
Bartlesville, Oklahoma

Hillside is a large L plan, with a two-story living room and
master bedroom overlooking the L. A hipped roof blends
house and sky. There has been one addition, a playroom
by William Wesley Peters, vice-president of the Frank
Lloyd Wright Foundation. Harold Price, Jr., is the son of
Harold Price, Sr., who commissioned the Price Company
Tower (355).

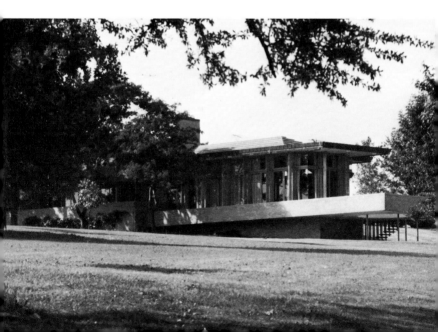

364 Lewis H. **Goddard** Residence (1953)
Plymouth, Michigan

An extended carport (not shown in the photograph) makes
this brick and wood house into an L plan. It is turned east-
southeast to gather the morning sun into the living room.
It is adjacent to "Snowflake" (281).

365 Louis **Penfield** Residence (1953)
Willoughby Hills, Ohio

Mr. Penfield's first house by Wright is of concrete block and
wood. Sleeping quarters are over kitchen facilities, both adjacent to the two-story living room, which looks through a
wooded hillside to the Chagrin River in the valley below.
From springtime floods, Mr. Penfield gathers stone, which
will go into the building of Wright's second house design for
this client, to be located southeast of the present structure.

366 Abraham **Wilson** (Bachman-Wilson) Residence (1954)
Millstone, New Jersey

Perhaps the idea for this house dates back to the 1941 project for the Ellinwood family. Like the Penfield house, it is of concrete block and wood with a two-story living room and sleeping quarters over the kitchen. The house was added to in 1970, on the north (at the left and outside of the photograph).

367 Wisconsin River Development Corporation, **Riverview Terrace Restaurant**, "The Spring Green," for W. H. Keland, president (1953)
Spring Green, Wisconsin

Perched on a hillside opposite Taliesin and just above the left bank of the Wisconsin River, this structure is the only restaurant designed by Wright that still stands today. Steel trusses were obtained from the flight deck of the aircraft carrier Ranger. Limestone, stucco, and various woods, including red oak paneling, are used. Originally "The Spring Green" was offered to the town Wright so dearly loved as a gift, and construction was begun by the Taliesin Fellowship in 1957. Halted for a variety of reasons, notably Wright's death, the project was again taken up in the late sixties. In a modified form, it was completed by the Taliesin Associated Architects as the first building in the Wisconsin River Development Corporation's planned resort adjacent to Taliesin. The restaurant is open during luncheon and dinner hours.

368 Willard H. **Keland** Residence (1954)
Racine, Wisconsin

The various wings of this structure create an atrium over which the two-story bedroom wing presides. This inner courtyard is, however, as much the creation of John H. Howe as of Wright, for it is the product of this Taliesin Fellow's 1961-designed playroom, greenhouse, and patio fountain addition (all on side opposite that shown in the photograph). Brick inside and out is laid under a copper roof. Mr. Keland is president of the Wisconsin River Development Corporation, which commissioned the Riverview Terrace Restaurant (367). Mrs. Keland is the daughter of H. F. Johnson, who built the Johnson Administration Building and Research Tower (237, 238) and Wingspread (239).

369, 370 **New York Usonian Exhibition House** and **Pavilion** (1953)
New York, New York
Demolished

After opening in the Palazzo Strozzi, Florence, and touring
Europe, the exhibit "Sixty Years of Living Architecture"
came to New York City. It was housed in the Usonian Exhibition House, on the site of the current Guggenheim
Museum (400).

371 Ellis A. **Feiman** Residence (1954)
Canton, Ohio

This wood-trimmed, brick structure is based on the 1953
New York Usonian Exhibition House (369). Its terrace/
lanai is fully open to the sun, while the roof skylight overhangs just enough to shade the living room in the summer
yet admit light in the winter. The Feiman residence is, in
interior space, an L plan, but the carport alters this to a
pinwheel. It is located near both the Rubin (343) and
Dobkins (362) houses.

372 Maurice **Greenberg** Residence, "Stonebroke" (1954)
Dousman, Wisconsin

Still not completed, the Greenberg residence cantilevers
from the brow of its hill. Originally designed, like Taliesin,
in native stone, it was finally built in brick, concrete, and
wood.

373 **Beth Sholom Synagogue** (1954)
Elkins Park, Pennsylvania

This edifice of concrete, steel, aluminum, glass, fiberglass, and oiled walnut is suspended from a tripod frame that allows the full upper floor complete freedom from internal supports. A separate chapel is directly below. The synagogue was dedicated on September 20, 1959. Tours are conducted most days, and a booklet explaining the design of the building is also available. This structure has been designated by the American Institute of Architects as one of seventeen American buildings designed by Frank Lloyd Wright to be retained as an example of his architectural contribution to American culture.

374 E. Clarke **Arnold** Residence (1954)
Columbus, Wisconsin

The Arnold residence is built in native stone from the Sauk
City area of Wisconsin. Originally of two wings set at 120
degrees to each other on a diamond module, its plan is now
a Y by the 1959 addition of a wing designed by John H.
Howe.

375 John E. **Christian** Residence (1954)
West Lafayette, Indiana

This brick and wood single-story house sits on a small hill near Purdue Stadium. The plan includes a walled garden on the northeast, the only part of this four-foot-square module structure to employ a circular segment, southeast living room (right in the photograph) and central work space under a clerestory. This clerestory has a fascia of copper; the lower fascia of wood is to be surfaced with a three-dimensional design constructed of copper.

376 Louis B. **Fredrick** Residence (1954)
Barrington Hills, Illinois

The Fredrick house commands the top of one of the Barrington Hills, nestling just below its crest. The roofline, instead of reaching outward as it rises, recedes to admit light. Mrs. Fredrick notes that the contractor's placement of the foundation, only a few degrees from Wright's designation, caused the light to shine much more deeply into the living room than had been intended. Three bedrooms, living room, work space, guest-playroom, and two galleries are enclosed by buckskin range brick and Philippine mahogany.

377 I. N. **Hagan** Residence (1954)
Chalkhill, Pennsylvania

From just below the peak of Kentuk Knob, the Hagan
house appears to grow out of the hillside. At the opposite
extremity, it is a ship's prow sailing the Pennsylvania Highlands. From above, it is part of the hill; from below, a strik-
ing complement to it. It employs hexagonal modules, completely eliminating right angles from the plan. Construction
materials are primarily native sandstone quarried at the site
and Tidewater red cypress.

378 Harold Price, Sr., Residence, "Grandma House" (1954)
Paradise Valley, Arizona

The central room, which divides the I plan into wings, is an atrium whose roof, raised on pylons, creates an open clerestory to admit fresh breezes. This same roof provides shade from the desert sun and shelter from flash thunderstorms, yet its open skylight admits sun to play on the water in the central fountain. Concrete block is used throughout. Mr. Price also commissioned the Price Company Tower (355).

379   Cedric G. **Boulter** Residence (1954) and
379A   **Addition** (1958)

The Boulter house is of concrete block and wood, the latter stained Taliesin red. As is the common practice in Wright houses, the module is marked out in the Taliesin red-colored cement floor, squares equal to three concrete blocks on a side. A balcony juts into the two-story-high living room from second-story bedrooms, its west extension becoming an exterior balcony. The terrace retaining wall is battered. A technique used in nearly all masonry work on Wright houses is apparent in the laying of the block; grouting in vertical joints is flush with the surface, while in horizontal joints it is normally recessed. This emphasizes the horizontal nature of the structure. An addition to the house by Wright is not recorded in the Taliesin archives. Wright's plan took the addition beyond the property line. Supervisor of construction, Benjamin Dombar, revised this to meet building codes and obtained approval from Wright for the changes.

380 Hoffman Auto Showroom (1954)
New York, New York

This interior remodeling of the ground-floor northeast corner of a New York City curtain wall skyscraper was done for Maximilian Hoffman (390). At the time, Hoffman was an importer of the British Jaguar; the showroom has since been used as a New York office of Mercedes-Benz. The ramp (to the left in the photograph) curves around the main circle of the display floor. Posts of the skyscraper are surfaced with mirrors, as are some walls.

381 Frank Lloyd Wright, **Hotel Plaza Apartment Remodeling** (1954)
New York, New York
Demolished, 1968

Wright remodeled an apartment in the Hotel Plaza to use for visits to New York City while the Guggenheim Museum and other New York and Connecticut projects were under construction. While apprentices at Taliesin were building the necessary furniture, painted in black lacquer with red edges, Wright was having long red velvet curtains hung the full height of the high-ceilinged room. Rose-colored borders framed Japanese gold paper panels that were placed on the walls. Circular mirrors became part of the semicircular window arches. Crystal balls were attached to cord pendants, which, when pulled, turned on the mirror lights. The Wrights last stayed in this second-story apartment, known to some as "Taliesin the Third," on January 27, 1959.

382 Los Angeles Exhibition Pavilion (1954)
Los Angeles, California

In 1951 the exhibit "Sixty Years of Living Architecture"
opened in the Palazzo Strozzi, Florence. From there it went
to Zurich, Paris, Munich, Rotterdam, Mexico City, New
York City (369, 370), and, finally, Los Angeles. Here, the
pavilion was built contiguous to the Barnsdall Hollyhock
House (208). During the refurbishing of Hollyhock House
in the 1970s, the pavilion has been largely demolished.

383 John L. **Rayward** (Rayward-Shepherd) Residence, "Tirranna" (1955)
New Canaan, Connecticut

Tirranna—an Australian aboriginal word meaning "running waters"—is an intricate intermingling of the ellipse and the square in a four-foot module. A concrete block of Wright's design combines with Philippine mahogany and glass to create a house, swimming pool, and pond wedded to the Noroton River and its surrounding hills. The swimming pool splits in half the eighteen-foot drop from living room to pond, where a dam creates a waterfall. A series of fish steps at the far end of the dam provides for passage of fish through the twenty acres of woodland property. Landscaped by Frank Okamura, landscape architect of the Brooklyn Botanical Garden, and Charles Middeleer, the grounds contain such a quantity and variety of flora as to qualify as a major botanical garden. While the built-in and free-standing furniture, fabric designs, and carpet layout are of Wright's design, with the assistance of John deKoven Hill, there is also a treehouse for children designed by Taliesin Associated Architects' chief architect, William Wesley Peters. Though originally designed for Mr. Rayward, H. R. Shepherd brought the design to completion. (Photograph by Carol Ruth Shepherd.)

384 William L. **Thaxton** Residence (1954)
Bunker Hill, Texas

Deep among the tall oaks west of Houston sits this battered,
concrete-block-walled, triangular-moduled house. The detailing in the fascia alone contains over nine hundred pieces
of trim. The 60-degree L plan encloses a swimming pool.
There is an addition, not by Wright, which is detached from
the main dwelling.

385 Randall **Fawcett** Residence (1955)
Los Banos, California

Battered concrete block and angles of 120 and 60 degrees
form the basis of this house. Its two wings each make a 60-
degree angle to the main space, which contains the entry
and a large living room space with walk-in fireplace. A modern version of the shallow, circular flower planter so often
favored by Wright is shown on the right in the photograph.

386 Gerald B. **Tonkens** Residence (1954)
Amberley Village, Ohio

A major statement in the history of Usonian automatic
houses, this residence sits on six acres atop a knoll. Pierced
blocks admit light to the work space core as a clerestory.
This core contains heating and cooling units raised above
floor level and other utilities. One wall of the core is the
living room fireplace. The L plan of the interior space
makes its 90-degree turn around the work space; the living
room, extended by a lanai, is the short L leg; sleeping quarters and study are in the longer leg. In the exterior plan, a
second L develops by way of a cantilevered carport at 90
degrees to the bedroom wing. The house is constructed on
a two-foot-square module with the standard wall block surface two feet by one foot. Wood for both paneling and
furniture is Philippine mahogany. The care exercised in the
seventeen-months-long construction of this dwelling is evident. Eric Wright, a grandson of the architect, supervised
construction from engineering drawings by William Wesley
Peters. Other supervisors included Thomas Casey and John
deKoven Hill (fabrics and furniture). John H. Howe assisted
Wright with the original drawings. As is common in Usonian
blocks, the interior surface is coffered. Engineering of the
block and reinforced-steel ceiling was by Mendel Glickman—
the only non-Taliesin principal on the project—in collaboration with Peters and the architect. Hill and Cornelia Brierly
designed the landscaping.

387 Toufic H. **Kalil** Residence (1955)
Manchester, New Hampshire

This is a Usonian automatic house of L or, with carport, T plan. There are no large windows; light is admitted through the pierced block, and the house is turned southwest to northeast to shade the patio in the afternoon.

388 Dorothy H. **Turkel** Residence (1955)
Detroit, Michigan

The pierced, light-admitting blocks around the two-story
living room—which faces south and east—are much larger
than those of the Kalil house (387), thus maintaining a
proper sense of scale in this larger house. Usonian automatic construction was employed in this L-plan structure.

389 W. B. **Tracy** Residence (1955)
Normandy Park, Washington

This Usonian automatic house nestles into a rise just above
the cliff on the east shore of Puget Sound. Though the
blocks appear to be uniform, they are of several forms for
inside and outside corner, roof, and walls.

390 Maximilian **Hoffman Residence** (1955)
Rye, New York

The large living room of the Hoffman dwelling (visible in
the photograph) looks north and east over a swimming pool
and lawn to Long Island Sound. Kitchen and bedrooms are
south of this room, the bedrooms opening onto the yard.
The leg of the L plan covers the entrance to the grounds on
the back side of the house and continues into the garage
and servant quarters. Stone, plaster, and cedar shakes are
trimmed with a copper fascia. In 1972 Mrs. Martin Fisher
contracted with the Taliesin Associated Architects for the
addition of a wing. (Photograph by Ezra Stoller © ESTO,
courtesy of Mrs. Martin Fisher.)

391 Donald **Lovness Residence** (1955)
Stillwater, Minnesota

This stone and wood residence is one of the last Usonian houses. Wright's first drawings showed an even rhythm; the final ones articulated the facade by regressed corner windows, full-bay plate glass and half-bay doors, with clerestory blocked out in places for emphasis. The living room behind this facade includes workspace under the high roof, while master and guest bedrooms each form separate wings, completely eliminating the usual tunnel gallery. The Lovnesses also built a cottage (A435) from plans drawn up by Wright in 1958 and complemented it with furniture constructed on the first designs for the Barnsdall Hollyhock House.

392 T. A. **Pappas** Residence (1955)
Saint Louis, Missouri

In the rolling hills west of metropolitan Saint Louis sits this
salmon-tinted block house. It is a Usonian automatic unit
whose masonry structure could be built from blocks—
Wright called them "stones"—assembled by the client. So
this is precisely what the young clients did. Picking up
where the prime contractor left off, with the walls only
partly finished, Bette and Ted completed their home, after
four years work, in 1964. Family resemblance among
Wright's block houses is strong, even when two dozen different stone forms are employed, as here. The fascia block,
otherwise shaped like that of the Tonkens residence (386),
in this instance opens its "U" design up. When building
development adjacent to the site for which the building was
designed proved unsuitable, the house was set in another
locale, graded to suit Wright's intent and rotated 180 degrees for the available view. The master bedroom is placed
immediately next the workspace, and the three children's
rooms, clustered side by side, complete the bedroom wing
without the need of the more usual, lengthy, tunnel gallery.

393 Robert H. **Sunday** Residence (1955)
Marshalltown, Iowa

A brick structure with wood fascia and trim, this L plan
was transformed into a T by an addition made in 1970
from 1969 plans of John H. Howe. This is possibly the last
of the brick Usonian homes. It faces southwest down its
hillside site, and its living room views three compass directions.

394 Warren **Scott Remodeling** of the **Isabel Roberts** Residence
(1955)
River Forest, Illinois

The Scott remodeling of the Isabel Roberts house (150)
involved brick veneer resurfacing, with blonde Philippine
mahogany in the interior. The east rooms of the lower level
have also been converted to a study by the Scotts.

395 Dallas Theatre Center (1955)
Dallas, Texas

The Dallas Theatre Center—locally also called the Kalita
Humphreys Theater—is of concrete in cantilever construction, with a 127-ton, concrete stage loft. The circular stage
drum, extending well above the rest of the concrete mass,
is the focus of the design, which, aside from circles, employs
modules with 60- and 120-degree angles. The 40-foot circular stage, within the drum, itself contains a 32-foot turn-
table. The theater can seat 404 people in eleven rows. The
terrace above the foyer (at left in the photograph) has been
enclosed to provide studio space and the foyer extended,
giving a more monumental feeling to the once-light entrance
wing. Tours are conducted daily.

THE KALITA HUMPHREYS THEATER

396 Karl **Kundert Medical Clinic** (1955)
San Luis Obispo, California

A brick structure, this clinic is of L plan with its terrace enclosed by both the L and the retaining wall above the adjacent creek bed. Offices and laboratory facilities are in opposite wings off the central reception room below the clerestory. This clerestory is made of pierced wood panels with glass inset; such panels were used often by Wright in wood structures to admit patterned light, for example, in the Wilson residence (366). A similar principle underlies the pierced blocks of block houses, such as the Tonkens and Kalil residences (386, 387).

397 Kenneth L. **Meyers Medical Clinic** (1956)
Dayton, Ohio
This clinic's reception room is at one end of the 120-degree-
angled structure (in the foreground of the photograph),
with doctors' rooms at the other.

398 Paul J. **Trier** Residence (1956)
Des Moines, Iowa

The living room (at right in the photograph) of this wood-trimmed brick structure faces south-southwest, opening on-to a terrace. For additional space, the Taliesin Associated Architects added a north wing in 1967.

399 Annunciation **Greek Orthodox Church** (1956)
Wauwatosa, Wisconsin

Form and structure, function and symbolism are here
united in integral expression with religious purpose. The
roof form and structure of this church is a concrete shell
dome originally surfaced in blue ceramic mosaic tile, the
tile later replaced by a synthetic plastic resin similar to that
of the Marin County Civic Center (416-417). The roof
dome is supported by reinforced-concrete cylindrical truss-
ing, visually expressed in the balcony-level fenestration
pattern. In turn, the truss is held aloft by four concrete
piers that are created by the terminals of the inward-curving
concrete walls that form a Greek cross in the plan at the
main level. The balcony further unifies the composition. Its
disc-like shape has outer edges that are gravity-supported by
the circular truss that it helps to laterally stabilize. The
basement is open space, adaptable to the varied needs of
the congregation. It opens on to sunken-level gardens. The
church is open to visitors.

400 Solomon R. **Guggenheim Museum** (1956)
New York, New York

The main gallery of the Guggenheim is a continuous spiraling inclined ramp in concrete. Wright intended this spiral incline to counteract the usual dominance of right-angled architecture over the flat plane of a picture. He also intended visitors to take the elevator to the top of the spiral, then walk down to the ground floor. Overcoming the restrictions of the New York City building code took more time than design and construction, but the original design of 1943, labeled a "ziggurat," is still evident in the final plan. The museum is open daily and Sunday for a small admission charge. This structure has been designated by the American Institute of Architects as one of seventeen American buildings designed by Frank Lloyd Wright to be retained as an example of his architectural contribution to American culture.

401 Wyoming Valley Grammar School (1956)
Wyoming Valley, Wisconsin

Not far south of Taliesin is this school, the only public ele-
mentary schoolhouse built from a Wright design. It is of
concrete block and redwood with shingled roof. Employing
60- and 120-degree angles in its plan, it is actually a two-
room school with central loggia. The large rooms are skylighted, and each has its own fireplace. The building is open
when school is in session.

402 Dudley Spencer Residence (1956)
Wilmington, Delaware

Stone predominates inside and out in this structure. The
hemicycle-plan living room facade opens onto a terrace.
(Drawing delineated by Harvey Ferrero.)

403 Allen Friedman Residence (1956)
Bannockburn, Illinois

This is one of the few Y-plan houses by Wright. Utilizing 60- and 120-degree angles throughout, the wings house living room, sleeping quarters, and carport, intersecting at the entry and kitchen area. The built-in, and much of the free-standing, furniture is by Wright. The Friedmans received their final plan revisions just before Wright's death.

404 Frank **Bott** Residence (1956)
Kansas City, Missouri

The terne metal roof of the Bott residence seems to grow
out of the crest of the hill over which one approaches the
house. The living room and balcony cantilever far out over
the hill toward the left bank of the Missouri River, affording the Botts a lovely view of Kansas City and providing
complete privacy from neighbors that crowd the narrow
lot. Construction is desert rubblestone wall, employing one
mile of farmer's wall stone from nearby flinthills in Kansas
and Philippine mahogany on a four-foot module.

Of four prefabricated house designs by Wright for the Marshall Erdman Company, only two were ever constructed. This is the first. All five units built from this plan are virtually identical in their L plans but differ in detail. Each has a masonry core, with painted, horizontal board and batten siding on the bedroom wing. The living room is below the entryway at the inner intersection of the L, and kitchen-dining facilities are in the short leg, with attached garage or carport. All have a utilities space basement; the Jackson, Iber and Post houses complete this into a full basement. The Van Tamelen is of concrete block; the Jackson and Iber are of stone; and the Post and Cass employ brick.

VanTamelen Residence

Jackson Residence, "Skyview"

Iber Residence

Post Residence

Cass Residence, "The Crimson Beech"

411 Joseph **Mollica** Residence (1956)
Bayside, Wisconsin
This stone dwelling was constructed from a plan that is a
mirror image of the Erdman units (406-410).

412, 413 Marshall Erdman Company, **Prefab #2** (1957)

412 Walter **Rudin** Residence
Madison, Wisconsin

This second of the four prefab designs for Marshall Erdman is the "one-room house." It is essentially a square plan. The large two-story living room (on the right in the photograph) is overlooked by a balcony outside the second-story sleeping quarters. The two units built are both of concrete block and painted, horizontal board and batten. The Rudin house is the original model and is situated on a flat site. This version of the one-room house is a wood structure based on the textile-block Usonian automatic type A for Walter Bimson of the Valley National Bank, Arizona.

Marshall Erdman Company, Prefab #2
413 James B. **McBean** Residence
Rochester, Minnesota

The McBean residence is set into a hillside site and so angled
as to take maximum advantage of the sun both morning
and afternoon.

414 R. W. **Lindholm Service Station** (1956)
Cloquet, Minnesota

This is a cement-block structure, painted, with terne metal roof and cantilevered canopy. The design derives from the Broadacre City Standardized Overhead Service Station of 1932, except that ground-based fuel pumps are used instead of the overhead fuel lines as envisioned by Wright. This is the only service station constructed from Wright's designs. Its service waiting room (in center of photograph) is over the attendants' area, while mechanics' working areas are on ground level.

415 **Marin County** Civic Center, **Post Office** (1957)
San Raphael, California

Wright's only constructed work for the United States Government is this building in the Marin County Civic Center. A nearly circular structure of concrete block and forms, this post office sits at the foot of the hill below the Marin County Administration Building (416). Nearby is a Taliesin-designed theater. Former Taliesin Fellow and San Francisco architect Aaron Green supervised all these government projects. The post office is open during regular office hours.

416 **Marin County** Civic Center, **Administration Building** and
417 **Hall of Justice** (1957)
San Raphael, California

Few were the buildings designed by Wright for governmental agencies, and fewer still were those that were built, namely only those in Marin County. The Marin County Civic Center includes a main Administration Building and contiguous Hall of Justice of similar concrete forms and terne metal roof. Reaching out from the domed library center, behind the eye-commanding pylon (functionally a radio antenna), each of these wings seeks a distant hill, complementing the spaces between them. The plastic membrane over the concrete roof covers three single-story arcades. The buildings are open to visitors during regular business hours.

418 Wichita State University, **Juvenile Cultural Study Center**
(1957)
Wichita, Kansas

Cast concrete, metals, and much glass constitute the two
rectangular units either side of a patio that together com-
prise the first (Building A) of two works designed by Wright
for this project. Both units are two stories high, with class-
rooms and office space, and courtyards symmetrically
placed about the patio axis. The buildings, also known as
the Harry F. Corbin Education Center, after the president
of Wichita State University at the time of construction, are
open to visitors during regular university session hours.

419 C. E. **Gordon** Residence (1957)
Aurora, Oregon
Wright's only work in Oregon is this concrete-block structure of T plan. The two-story living room (in the foreground of the photograph) runs north to the south bank
of the Willamette River, opening to both east and west
views. Bedrooms, with balconies, are in the head of the T,
over kitchen and work spaces.

420 Duey Wright Residence (1957)
Wausau, Wisconsin

Concrete block is here used to create the circular section of
a living room that commands a westward view from high
above the left bank of the Wisconsin River. Approximately
an L plan, the design is said to imitate a musical note. The
kitchen is adjacent to the living room, while sleeping quarters are in the long wing with a carport at its end. Duey
Wright is not related to the architect.

421 Robert G. **Walton** Residence (1957)
Modesto, California

Situated near a south bank of the Stanislaus River, this concrete-block house with wood fascia and trim is of T plan. The south bedroom and east living room wings open to easterly views across the broad river basin from the low hillside site, opposite the entry shown in the photograph.

422 **Sterling Kinney** Residence (1957)
Amarillo, Texas

Battered red brick walls at all but the living room facades
(as shown in the photograph) characterize this house set on
the cap rock of the west Texas panhandle. A T plan, its
kitchen separates the living room and sleeping quarters,
opening both to the bedroom porch and the main living
space. A separate porch forms an L around the west and
north facades of the sunken living room, shown in the photograph above the goldfish pond.

423 Private Residence (1957)
Indian Hill, Ohio
This is an L-plan, brick structure. (Rendering by Harvey
Ferrero.)

424 Herman T. **Fasbender Medical Clinic**, Mississippi Valley
Clinic (1957)
Hastings, Minnesota

Formerly a medical clinic and now business offices, this
brick structure is given added character by the draping of
its terne metal roof.

425 Lockridge Medical Clinic, for Drs. Lockridge, McIntyre, and Whalen (1958)
Whitefish, Montana

A rectangular building, this former clinic is of brick, horizontal painted wood sheathing around the skylight, and concrete fascia. It has been converted into a bank and is open during regular business hours.

426 Carl **Schultz** Residence (1957)
Saint Joseph, Michigan
Pavement brick from the streets of nearby Benton Harbor
combines with mahogany trim in this house. Its living room
terrace (at left in the photograph) cantilevers out over a
ravine off the left bank of the Saint Joseph River.

427 Paul **Olfelt** Residence (1958)
Saint Louis Park, Minnesota

Triangular forms mold sleeping quarters into a hillside,
open the living room to a view downhill, and fit the whole
into the only level part of the terrain.

428 George **Ablin** Residence (1958)
Bakersfield, California

Salmon concrete block, cedar shingles, and wood trim are combined in this house on a knoll next to the Bakersfield Country Club. The living room opens to the southeast, its view protected from nearby development.

429 Don M. **Stromquist** Residence (1958)
Bountiful, Utah

Wright's only work in Utah is a concrete-block structure
built on a triangular module. No other dwellings exist within a half-mile in any direction, and the structure, situated
halfway down the canyon wall, looks south to wooded wilderness. The master bedroom features a balcony that
reaches out over the canyon valley, and the living room, a
terrace, both triangular. (Photograph courtesy of Ray R.
Schofield.)

430 Seth **Petersen** Residence (1958)
Lake Delton, Wisconsin

Native stone and wood are used in this "one-room cottage"
on the ledge above the south shore of Mirror Lake. The
fireplace is central to the square plan, its masonry dividing
the south half of the interior space in two. Acquired in the
1960s by the State of Wisconsin, it is on a fenced-in western limit of Mirror Lake State Park.

431 Pilgrim **Congregational Church** (1958)
Redding, California

Of desert rubblestone wall construction, this building was
not Taliesin-supervised during construction and remains un-
finished today. The main roof is suspended from concrete
bents. The building is usually open during weekdays.

432 Arizona State University, Grady **Gammage Memorial Auditorium** (1959)
Tempe, Arizona

The last nonresidential design by Wright to be constructed is this auditorium that seats 3000 persons continental style (that is, with wide spacing between rows and no center aisle). There are 50 concrete columns cast on the site, and each rises 55 feet to support the outer roof, whose deck is gypsum and thin-shell concrete with a roofing of composition and sprayed-on asphalt. The exterior walls are brick and marblecrete (a marblelike composition material) in desert-rose finish; interior brick and sand finish plaster with acoustical tile. Walnut trim and reinforced-concrete floors complete the list of major construction materials. The grand tier is suspended forward of the rear auditorium wall on a 145-foot-long steel beam—a unique solution to the acoustical problems of a seating space between orchestra and balcony. No smoking is permitted in lobby or auditorium—there were intentionally no provisions made for ash trays. Tours are conducted daily. (Photograph courtesy of Arizona State University.)

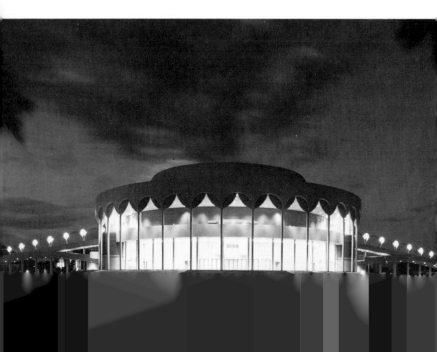

433 Norman **Lykes** Residence (1959)
Phoenix, Arizona

This is the last residential design by Wright to be built. Taliesin Fellow John Rattenbury did the detail work and furniture and supervised construction, which took place during 1966-1968. The living room is of circular plan, and all other parts of the total plan are circular segments. Dessert-rose concrete block and Philippine mahogany are the materials employed. The second-floor study above the living room drum is an alteration to the plan made by Rattenbury.

ADDENDA

Wright-designed structures are still being built. Whether it be an original client now able to afford the project, or a person willing to build something suitable to his needs and site that was designed for another client and location, the Taliesin Associated Architects (TAA) engineer Wright's plans and elevations with modern appurtenances and provide necessary construction supervision. This continues the tradition practiced in Wright's lifetime.

The first date listed with each project is that of the concept as first drawn by Wright, whomever the client. Successive datings indicate when TAA engineered actual construction plans.

A434 Arthur and Bruce Brooks **Pfeiffer** Residence (1938-1974)
Scottsdale, Arizona

The Ralph Jester home, on which this design was based,
was one of Wright's favorite concepts. It was his reaction to
the capabilities of plywood, not as a cheaper, but as a more
plastic, wood. The Jester design was for the sea breezes of
Palos Verdes, California. Wright developed this idea through
several versions in various materials and for many sites;
Gerald M. Loeb (1944) in Redding, Connecticut, and Dr.
Paul V. Palmer (1947) in Phoenix, Arizona, being notable.
The Pfeiffer home sits on the east edge of Taliesin West. It
features flamingo quartz trowelled into wet concrete, and
proportions enlarged to accommodate the height of Frank
Lloyd Wright Memorial Foundation archivist Bruce Brooks
Pfeiffer and his father Arthur. A carport forms an added
wing to the basic Jester plan.

A435 Donald and Virginia **Lovness Cottage** (1958-1976)
Stillwater, Minnesota

This and the Seth Petersen cottage (430) were built from the same basic plan. Here, however, no compromise was allowed in plan or materials. The butterfly roof projection was engineered by William Wesley Peters. A full basement foundation was required by the sandy, hilly site above Woodpile Lake. Furnishings are from the first designs by Wright for Aline Barnsdall's Hollyhock House (208).

A436 Hilary and Joe **Feldman** Residence (1939-1974)
Berkeley, California

This house is based on the Lewis N. Bell project. It features
a full terrace with adjacent pavilion opening directly to the
workspace. Thirty thousand bricks were specially made to
the 2 1/4″ Eastern U.S., rather than the 2 5/8″ California,
standard to fit Wright's 13″ unit system, here applied to a
two-foot-grid parallelogram module. California clearheart
redwood is used in the board and batten walls and for trim.
This is the predecessor to the Carlton D. Wall house (281).
(Photograph courtesy of Joshua Freiwald.)

A437 **First Christian Church** (1950-1971/1977)
Phoenix, Arizona

Wright's presentation drawings of a university campus for the Southwest Christian Seminary were published in August 1951. In October of the following year, under the leadership of Dr. William S. Boice, the Congregation of the First Christian Church was founded. When plans for the university did not materialize, permission was granted for the building of the chapel, then other segments of the project, by the First Christian Church. Initial stages of construction were completed from 1971 to 1973. The work is set on concrete piers, and reveals native desert stone in rough concrete above ground. It has a roofing of blue urethane membrane, the seventies alternative to copper. The stained glass window, "Regenesis," is by John Amarantides of the Taliesin Fellowship. (Photograph courtesty of the First Christian Church.)

ILLUSTRATION CREDITS

The following photographs were reprinted from *Frank Lloyd Wright to 1910* by Grant Carpenter Manson, © 1958 by Litton Educational Publishing, Inc., by permission of Van Nostrand Reinhold Company.

The following photographs were reprinted from the collection of Henry-Russell Hitchcock.

PLANS

The plans presented in this volume represent the various periods of Wright's creative activity in residential design. Many demonstrate the basic plans employed by Wright; cruciform, L, and others are shown. Some show the basic modules and geometric forms with which Wright worked: the hexagon, octagon, triangle. Plans for the main floor only are shown, as examples of their types. Plans for the Winslow, Willits, Robie, Mrs. Millard, Kaufmann, First Jacobs, Herbert F. Johnson, McCartney, and Laurent residences are from the collection of Henry-Russell Hitchcock.

Winslow Residence (24)

This residence was Wright's first independent commission after leaving the firm of Adler & Sullivan. The plan is rectangular. The upper floor is sleeping quarters.

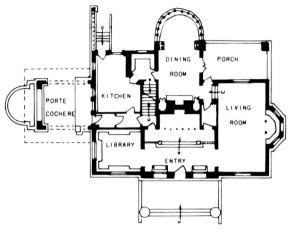

FIRST (MAIN) FLOOR PLAN

Husser Residence (46)

While looking back to an early form, the octagon, this house already suggests Prairie characteristics. The main floor is the second of three. The lower level was a "basement" raised to ground level. This ground-level basement was later to become a characteristic of the Prairie house, although here it may have been designed to prevent flooding of the lakeside structure. The house is essentially an I plan. The upper (third) floor was sleeping quarters.

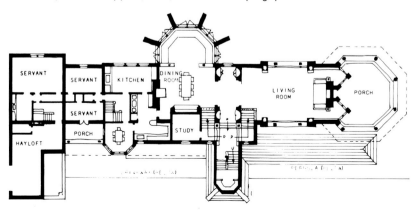

SECOND (MAIN) FLOOR PLAN

Willits Residence (54)

This is a major early Prairie house of pinwheel plan. Its
upper floor is sleeping quarters.

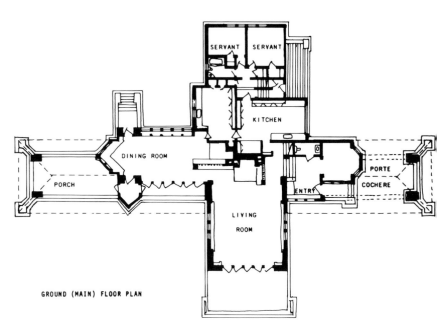

SERVANT SERVANT

KITCHEN

DINING ROOM

PORCH

PORTE
COCHERE

ENTRY

LIVING
ROOM

GROUND (MAIN) FLOOR PLAN

Robie Residence (127)

To many, this building is Wright's major statement in the Prairie idiom. The ground floor contains a billiards room below the living room and children's area below the dining room. The third floor is sleeping quarters. All three stories take no more height than most two-story houses of the same era.

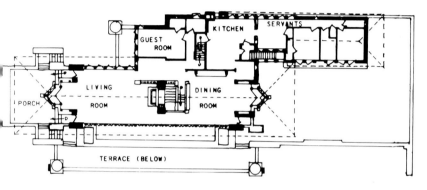

SECOND **(MAIN) FLOOR PLAN**

Mrs. Millard Residence (214)

One of the California block houses, this residence looks into a glen below its entrance (main) level. The lower level has the dining room below the main-level living room and also includes kitchen and storage spaces. The upper level has sleeping quarters and balcony, looking over the living room.

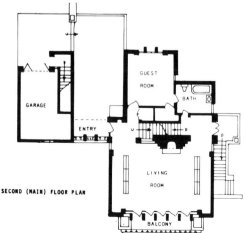

SECOND (MAIN) FLOOR PLAN

Kaufmann Residence, Fallingwater (230)

This house over a waterfall rises three stories, including living quarters and adjacent terraces, above the main level. Its living room is roughly square but so open to its terraces that it hardly seems enclosed. Despite its three stories, the house appears horizontal.

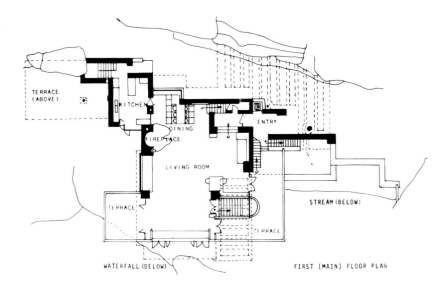

TERRACE (ABOVE)

KITCHEN

DINING

FIREPLACE

ENTRY

LIVING ROOM

TERRACE

STREAM (BELOW)

TERRACE

WATERFALL (BELOW)

FIRST (MAIN) FLOOR PLAN

First Jacobs Residence (234)

The first of hundreds of Usonian house designs to be built, the Jacobs house is of L plan on a rectangular module. It is set on concrete slab, through which heating pipes, conducting gravity heat, run. It contains only a utilities basement.

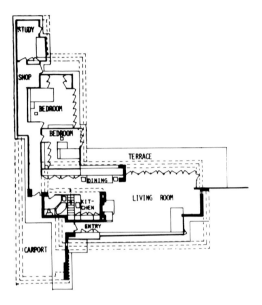

Hanna Honeycomb House (235)

The Hanna residence is built on a hexagonal module and curves around its hillside site.

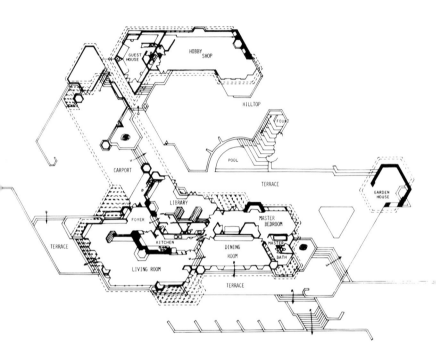

Herbert F. Johnson Residence, Wingspread (239)

The wings of this dwelling spread to the four compass directions from a central octagon. The result is the largest, and last, expression of the Prairie house in a plan that may be called modified cruciform but that is actually a pinwheel. It is also a fine example of the "zoned house," a dwelling with different activities relegated to specific areas—noisy activities separated from quiet, children from guests, servants from the master of the house.

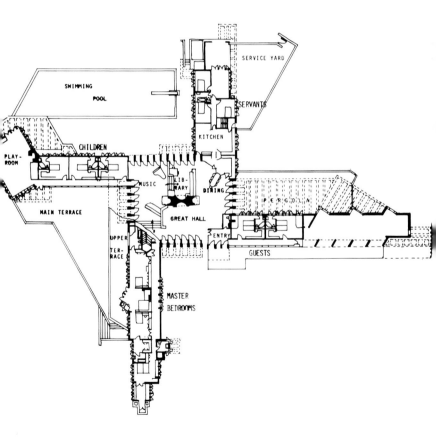

McCartney Residence (299)

The basic module of this Wright textile-block house is a
diamond, but that diamond results in many patterns. Half a
diamond is a equilateral triangle, and half of an equilateral
triangle is a right triangle; this latter configuration is clearly
apparent in the roofline. A later addition saw a new carport
beyond the work space entrance and the old carport made
into a bedroom.

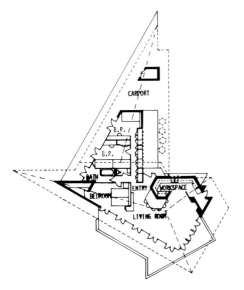

Laurent Residence (319)

Wright's first major expression in circular segments was the
second Jacobs residence, which had a single center for all
radii of the basic structure. In the Laurent dwelling, there
are two centers for circles that intersect. A later bedroom
addition is beyond the entry, next to the carport.

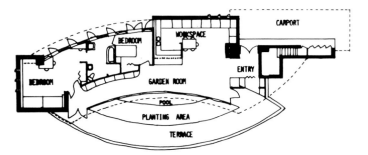

MAPS

In the seven maps here presented, one may trace the development of Wright's work over time and space. The last map shows the geographical distribution of all of Wright's opus. The other maps divide the constructed works into six time periods, with a dot for each extant constructed project or work and an x for each work of that period since demolished. Where the dots or x's are too numerous to distinguish in a given area, a figure indicates the number of works in that area.

1887-1898 Early Work: Eclectic and Original

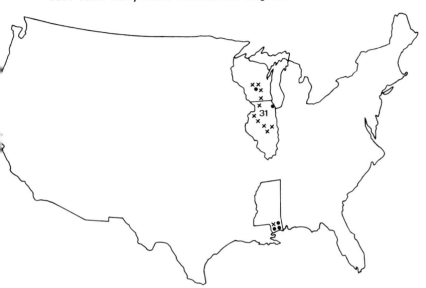

1899-1909 Coming of The Prairie House

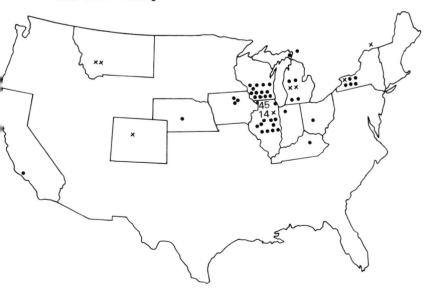

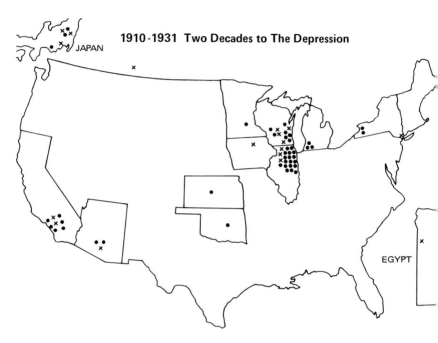

1910-1931 Two Decades to The Depression

JAPAN

EGYPT

1932-1942 Usonia I

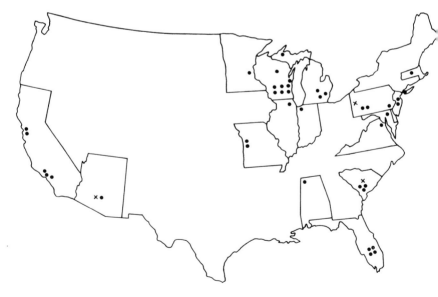

1943-1953 Of Hemicycles and . . .

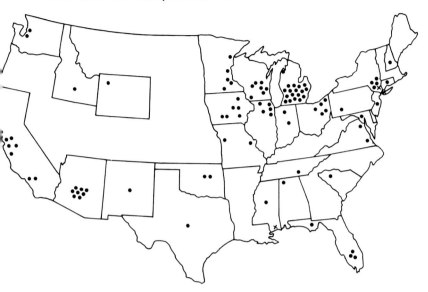

1954-1959 . . . Prefabs

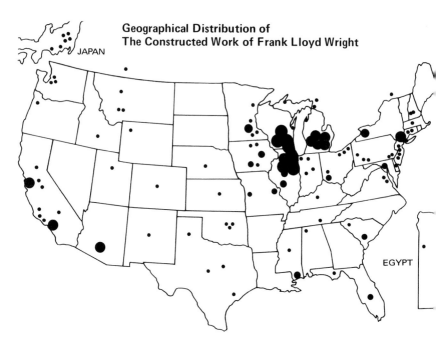

Geographical Distribution of
The Constructed Work of Frank Lloyd Wright

JAPAN

EGYPT

GEOGRAPHICAL INDEX BY ZIP CODE

The zip code system was devised by the Postal Service around geographically related distribution centers. Governmental units in generally contiguous regions share the first two or three digits of their given zip codes; i.e., 537xx is Madison, Wisconsin, including its suburbs (such as Shorewood Hills).

Readers may employ this sytem to locate structures known or remembered only by the general area in which they stand. For instance, one seeking a building somewhere around San Francisco, would look at all listings that have the same beginning zip numbers as that north California city. The 94xxx listings in this index include all extant structures designed by Wright in the Bay region.

The numbers in the right column refer to the catalog entry number, for ease of access to additional information concerning the item listed.

The alphabetical index lists structures by the city in which they were constructed or are currently located.

Zip code ranges, and relevant state listings, are:

00000-09999	Connecticut, Massachusetts, New Hampshire, New Jersey
10000-19999	Delaware, New York, Pennsylvania
20000-29999	Maryland, South Carolina, Virginia
30000-39999	Alabama, Florida, Mississippi, Tennessee
40000-49999	Kentucky, Michigan, Ohio
50000-59999	Iowa, Minnesota, Montana, Wisconsin
60000-69999	Illinois, Kansas, Missouri, Nebraska
70000-79999	Oklahoma, Texas
80000-89999	Arizona, Idaho, New Mexico, Utah, Wyoming
90000-99999	California, Oregon, Washington

Foreign listings follow the U.S. listings

Note: This geographical index of extant buildings is not meant to encourage visits to private homes. The privacy that Wright designed into his clients' residences must be respected. Buildings that are open to visitors are so noted in the text.

New York (*continued*)

14214	**Buffalo**	
	125 Jewett Pkwy.	**Darwin D. Martin Residence,** 100
	118 Summit Ave.	**Barton,** 103
	285 Woodward Ave.	**Darwin D. Martin Gardener's Cottage,** 132
14216	**Buffalo**	
	57 Tillinghast Pl.	**Davidson,** 149
14222	**Buffalo**	
	76 Soldiers Pl.	**Heath,** 105
14610	**Rochester**	
	16 East Blvd.	**Boynton,** 147

PA   Pennsylvania

15421	**Chalkhill**	
	Ohiopyle Rd.	**Hagan,** 377
15464	**Mill Run**	
	Bear Run	**Kaufmann Residence "Fallingwater," Guesthouse,** and **Guesthouse Alterations,** 230-232
18105	**Allentown**	**Little Residence II**
	Fifth and Court Streets	(library), 173
19003	**Ardmore**	
	152-158 Sutton Rd.	**Suntop Homes,** 248
19117	**Elkins Park**	
	Old York Rd. at Foxcroft	**Beth Sholom Synagogue,** 373

DE   Delaware

19809	**Wilmington**	
	619 Shipley Rd.	**Dudley Spencer,** 402

MD   Maryland

20034	**Bethesda**	
	7927 Deepwell Dr.	**Llewellyn Wright,** 358
21215	**Baltimore**	
	6807 Cross Country Blvd.	**Euchtman,** 270

VA   Virginia

22101	**McLean**	
	600 Chainbridge Rd.	**Luis Marden,** 357
22121	**Mount Vernon**	
	Woodlawn Plantation	**Pope,** 268
23455	**Virginia Beach**	
		Cooke, 360

SC   South Carolina

29609	**Greenville**	
	9 West Avondale Dr.	**Austin,** 345

Ohio (*continued*)

| 45237 | **Amberley Village** | |
| | 6980 Knoll Rd. | **Tonkens, 386** |

| 45243 | **Indian Hill** | |
| | | **Private Residence, 423** |

| 45429 | **Dayton** | |
| | 5441 Far Hills Ave. | **Meyers Medical Clinic, 397** |

| 45505 | **Springfield** | |
| | 1340 East High St. | **Westcott, 99** |

IN   Indiana

| 46368 | **Ogden Dunes** | |
| | Cedar Trail at The Ledge | **Armstrong, 260** |

| 46601 | **South Bend** | |
| | 715 West Washington St. | **DeRhodes, 125** |

| 46614 | **South Bend** | |
| | 1404 Ridgedale Rd. | **Mossberg, 302** |

| 46952 | **Marion** | |
| | 1119 Overlook Rd. | **Davis, 324** |

| 47906 | **West Lafayette** | |
| | 1301 Woodland Ave. | **Christian, 375** |

MI   Michigan

48013	**Bloomfield Hills**	
	5045 Pon Valley Rd.	**Melvyn Maxwell Smith, 287**
	1925 North Woodward Ave.	**Affleck, 274**

| 48104 | **Ann Arbor** | |
| | 227 Orchard Hills Dr. | **Palmer, 332** |

48170	**Plymouth**	
	12221 Beck Rd.	**Goddard, 364**
	12305 Beck Rd.	**Wall, 281**

| 48221 | **Detroit** | |
| | 2760 West Seven Mile Rd. | **Turkel, 388** |

48864	**Okemos**	
	2410 Hulett Rd.	**Goetsch-Winckler, 269**
	2504 Arrow Head Rd.	**Edwards, 313**
	2527 Arrow Head Rd.	**Brauner, 312**
	1155 Wrightwind Dr.	**Schaberg, 328**

49001	**Kalamazoo**	
	2662 Taliesin Dr.	**McCartney, 299**
	2806 Taliesin Dr.	**Eric V. Brown, 300**
	2816 Taliesin Dr.	**Levin, 298**
	2822 Taliesin Dr.	**Winn, 301**

| 49022 | **Benton Harbor** | |
| | 1150 Miami Rd. | **Anthony, 315** |

Michigan (*continued*)

49053	**Galesburg**	
	11036 Hawthorne Dr.	**Pratt**, 295
	11098 Hawthorne Dr.	**Eppstein**, 296
	11108 Hawthorne Dr.	**Meyer**, 297
	11185 Hawthorne Dr.	**Weisblat**, 294
49085	**Saint Joseph**	
	207 Sunnybank	**Harper**, 329
	2704 Highland Ct.	**Schultz**, 426
49117	**Grand Beach**	
	Crescent Rd.	**Vosburgh**, 197
	13303 Lakeview	**W. S. Carr**, 199
	13189 Lakeview	**Joseph J. Bagley**, 198
49416	**Whitehall**	
	5260 South Shore Dr.	**George Gerts**, 77
	5324 & 5370 South Shore	**Mrs. Thomas H. Gale**
	Drive	**Summer Residence** and
		Residence Duplicate I,
		88, 89
49503	**Grand Rapids**	
	450 Madison Ave. S.E.	**May**, 148
	505 College Ave. S.E.	**Amberg**, 166
49670	**Northport**	
	North Peterson Park Rd.	**Alpaugh**, 293
49754	**Marquette Island**	
	Les Cheneaux Club	**Heurtley Summer**
		Residence Remodeling, 75
49855	**Marquette**	
	Deertrack, County 492	**Abby Beecher Roberts**, 236

IA Iowa

50158	**Marshalltown**	
	Woodfield Rd.	**Sunday**, 393
50323	**Des Moines**	
	6880 North West Beaver Dr.	**Trier**, 398
50401	**Mason City**	
	West State St. at South	**City National Bank**
	Federal	**Building** and **Hotel**,
	West State St. at South	155, 156
	Enterprise	
	311 First St. S.E.	**Stockman**, 139
50616	**Charles City**	
	1107 Court St.	**Miller**, 289
52326	**Quasqueton**	
	Cedar Rock on	**Walter Residence** and
	Wapsipinicon River	**River Pavilion**, 284, 285
52403	**Cedar Rapids**	
	3400 Adel Dr. S.E.	**Grant**, 288
52577	**Oskaloosa**	
	1907 A Ave. East	**Alsop**, 304
	117 North Park Ave.	**Lamberson**, 305

WI Wisconsin

53115	**Lake Delavan**	
	3459 South Shore Dr.	**A. P. Johnson**, 87
	3409 South Shore Dr.	**Wallis Summer Residence**, 79
	3335 South Shore Dr.	**Fred B. Jones Residence, Gate Lodge, Barn with Stables,** and **Boathouse**, 83-86
	3211 South Shore Dr.	**Charles S. Ross**, 82
	3209 South Shore Dr.	**George W. Spencer**, 81
53118	**Dousman**	
	Highway 67	**Greenberg**, 372
53211	**Milwaukee**	
	2420 North Terrace Ave.	**Bogk**, 196
53215	**Milwaukee**	
	1835 South Layton Blvd.	**Richards Bungalow**, 203
	2714 West Burnham Blvd.	**Richards Small House**, 202
	2720-2732 West Burnham Blvd.	**Richards Duplex Apartments**, 201
53217	**Fox Point**	
	7111 North Barnett	**Albert Adelman**, 308
53217	**Bayside**	
	1001 West Jonathan	**Mollica**, 411
53225	**Wauwatosa**	
	North 92nd at West Congress St.	**Greek Orthodox Church**, 399
53402	**Wind Point**	
	33 East 4 Mile	**Herbert F. Johnson**, 239
53403	**Racine**	
	1525 Howe St.	**S. C. Johnson Administration Building** and **Research Tower**, 237, 238
	1319 South Main St.	**Hardy**, 115
53405	**Racine**	
	1425 Valley View Dr.	**Keland**, 368
53549	**Jefferson**	
	332 East Linden Dr.	**Richard Smith**, 337
53562	**Middleton**	
	7033 Old Sauk Rd.	**Jacobs Second Residence**, 283
53581	**Richland Center**	
	300 South Church St.	**German Warehouse**, 183
53588	**Wyoming Valley**	
	Route 23	**Wyoming Valley Grammar School**, 401

Wisconsin (*continued*)

53588	**Spring Green**	
	Route 23, Taliesin	**Taliesin Fellowship Complex,** 228
	Route 23, Taliesin	**Romeo and Juliet Windmill,** 37
	Route 23, Taliesin	**Porter,** 134
	Route 23, Taliesin	**Midway Barns** with **Dairy and Machine Sheds,** 246, 247
	Route 23, Taliesin	**Taliesin III** and **Dams** and **Enclosed Garden at Taliesin,** 218-220
	Route 23	**Riverview Terrace Restaurant,** 367
53703	**Madison**	
	22 North Butler St.	**Lamp Residence,** 97
53704	**Shorewood Hills**	
	3650 Mendota Dr.	**Pew,** 273
	900 University Bay Dr.	**Unitarian Church,** 291
53705	**Madison**	
	120 Ely Pl.	**Gilmore,** 146
	110 Marinette Trail	**Rudin,** 412
	5817 Anchorage Rd.	**VanTamelen,** 406
53711	**Madison**	
	441 Toepfer St.	**Jacobs First Residence,** 234
53713	**Madison**	
	2909 West Beltline Hwy.	**Jackson,** 407
53813	**Lancaster**	
	474 North Filmore St.	**Patrick Kinney,** 342
53925	**Columbus**	
	954 Dix St.	**Arnold,** 374
53940	**Lake Delton**	
	Hastings Rd.	**Petersen,** 430
54241	**Two Rivers**	
	3425 Adams	**Schwartz,** 271
54401	**Wausau**	
	904 Grand Ave.	**Duey Wright,** 420
	1224 Highland Park Blvd.	**Manson,** 249
54481	**Stevens Point**	
	Springville Dr. at U.S. 5	**Iber,** 408
54901	**Oshkosh**	
	1165 Algoma Blvd.	**Hunt Residence II,** 204

MN Minnesota

55033	**Hastings**	
	Minnesota 55 at Pine St.	**Fasbender Medical Clinic,** 424
55082	**Stillwater**	
	10121 83rd North	**Lovness Residence,** 391 and **Cottage,** A435

Minnesota (*continued*)

55414	**Minneapolis** 255 Bedford St. S.E.	**Willey**, 229
55416	**Minneapolis** 2801 Burnham Blvd.	**Neils**, 314
55416	**Saint Louis Park**	**Olfelt**, 427
55720	**Cloquet** Route 33 at Stanley Ave. Route 45 at Route 33	**Lindholm Residence**, 353 **Lindholm Service Station**, 414
55901	**Rochester** 22 Skyline Dr. S. W. 36 Skyline Dr. S. W. 1532 Woodland Dr. S. W.	**Bulbulian**, 292 **Keys**, 321 **McBean**, 413
55912	**Austin** 309 21st St. S. W.	**Elam**, 336

MT   Montana

59829	**Darby** Bunkhouse Rd.	**Como Orchard Summer Colony**, 144
59937	**Whitefish** 341 Central Ave.	**Lockridge Medical Clinic**, 425

IL   Illinois

60010	**Barrington Hills** 265 Donlea Rd. County Line Rd.	**Post**, 409 **Fredrick**, 376
60015	**Bannockburn** 200 Thornapple	**Allen Friedman**, 403
60022	**Glencoe** 790 Sheridan Rd. 850 Sheridan Rd. 1023 Meadow Rd. 1027 Meadow Rd. 1030 Meadow Rd. 1031 Meadow Rd. 272 Sylvan Rd. Sylvan Rd. 265 Sylvan Rd.	**Brigham**, 184 **Glasner**, 109 **Kissam**, 192 **William F. Ross**, 191 **Root**, 189 **Kier**, 190 **Perry**, 188 **Ravine Bluffs Development Sculptures and Bridge**, 185, 186 **Booth Residence**, 187
60025	**Glenview**	**John O. Carr**, 327
60035	**Highland Park** 1445 Sheridan Rd. 1689 Lake Ave. 1923 Lake Ave.	**Willits Residence** and **Gardener's Cottage with Stables**, 54, 55 **Millard**, 126 **Mary M. W. Adams**, 108

Illinois (*continued*)

60043	**Kenilworth**	
	205 Essex Rd.	**Baldwin,** 107
60045	**Lake Forest**	
	170 North Mayflower	**Glore,** 341
60048	**Libertyville**	
	153 Little Saint Mary's Rd.	**Lloyd Lewis Residence** and **Farm Unit,** 265, 266
60091	**Wilmette**	
	507 Lake Ave.	**Baker,** 151
60126	**Elmhurst**	
	301 South Kenilworth Ave.	**Henderson,** 57
60134	**Geneva**	
	1511 Batavia Rd.	**Fabyan Remodeling,** 129
	318 South Fifth	**Hoyt,** 120
60170	**Plato Center**	
	Rohrsen Rd.	**Muirhead,** 334
60202	**Evanston**	
	2420 Harrison St.	**Charles E. Brown,** 110
60302	**Oak Park**	
	404 Home Ave.	**George W. Smith,** 45
	Lake St. at Kenilworth Ave.	**Unity Church,** 96
	Lake St. at Oak Park	**Scoville Park Fountain,** 94
	Lake St. between Oak Park and North Euclid Ave.	**Francisco Terrace Apartments** (archway), 30
	210 Forest Ave.	**Thomas,** 67
	238 Forest Ave.	**Beachy,** 117
	6 Elizabeth Ct.	**Mrs. Thomas H. Gale Residence,** 98
	313 Forest Ave.	**Hills,** 51
	318 Forest Ave.	**Heurtley Residence,** 74
	333 Forest Ave.	**Moore Residence** and **Stable,** 34, 35
	400 Forest Ave.	**Copeland Residence Alterations,** 158
	408 Forest Ave.	**Copeland Garage,** 159
	428 Forest Ave.	**Frank Lloyd Wright Residence** and **Playroom Addition,** 2, 3
	951 Chicago Ave.	**Frank Lloyd Wright Studio,** 4 (**Nooker Restoration,** 405)
	1019 Chicago Ave.	**Thomas H. Gale,** 16
	1027 Chicago Ave.	**Parker,** 17
	1031 Chicago Ave.	**Walter M. Gale,** 20
	1030 Superior St.	**Wooley,** 23
	334 North Kenilworth Ave.	**Young Alterations,** 36
	611 North Kenilworth Ave.	**Balch,** 168
	223 North Euclid Ave.	**George Furbeck,** 43
	317 North Euclid Ave.	**Charles E. Roberts Stable Remodeling,** 41
	321 North Euclid Ave.	**Charles E. Roberts Residence Remodeling,** 40
	710 Augusta Ave.	**Harry S. Adams,** 179
	520 North East Ave.	**Cheney,** 104

Illinois (*continued*)

	534 North East Ave.	Goodrich, 42
	636 North East Ave.	William E. Martin Residence, 61
	515 Fair Oaks Ave.	Rollin Furbeck, 44
	540 Fair Oaks Ave.	Fricke Residence and Emma Martin Alterations and Garage, 58-60
60305	**River Forest**	
	Auvergne Pl. at Lake Ave.	Waller Gates, 65
	515 Auvergne Pl.	Winslow Residence and Stable, 24, 25
	530 Edgewood Pl.	Williams, 33
	603 Edgewood Pl.	Isabel Roberts, 150 (Scott Remodeling, 394)
	562 Keystone Ave.	Ingalls, 161
	559 Ashland Ave.	Davenport, 68
	615 Lathrop Ave.	River Forest Tennis Club, 119
60420	**Dwight**	
	122 West Main St.	Frank L. Smith Bank, 111
60422	**Flossmoor**	
	1136 Brassie Ave.	Nicholas, 118
60506	**Aurora**	
	1300 Garfield Ave.	Greene, 176
60510	**Batavia**	
	605 North Batavia Ave.	Gridley Residence, 121
60521	**Hinsdale**	
	121 County Line Rd.	Frederick Bagley, 28
60525	**LaGrange**	
	345 South Seventh Ave.	Hunt Residence I, 138
	108 South Eighth Ave.	Goan, 29
	109 South Eighth Ave.	Emmond, 15
60546	**Riverside**	
	300 Scottswood Rd.	Coonley Residence, 135
	290 Scottswood Rd.	Coonley Gardener's Cottage, 136
	336 Coonley Rd.	Coonley Coach House, 137
	350 Fairbanks Rd.	Coonley Playhouse, 174
	150 Nuttell Rd.	Tomek, 128
60604	**Chicago**	
	209 South LaSalle St.	Rookery Building Remodeling, 113
60610	**Chicago**	
	1365 Astor	Charnley Residence, 9
60612	**Chicago**	
	3005-3017 West Carroll Ave.	E-Z Polish Factory, 114
	2840-2858 West Walnut St.	Waller Apartments, 31

Illinois (*continued*)

60615	**Chicago**	
	1322 East 49th St.	**Blossom Garage,** 133
	4858 Kenwood Ave.	**Blossom Residence,** 14
	4852 Kenwood Ave.	**McArthur Residence, Residence Remodeling,** and **Stable,** 11-13
	5132 Woodlawn Ave.	**Heller,** 38
60616	**Chicago**	
	3213-3219 Calumet	**Roloson Apartments,** 26
60620	**Chicago**	
	9326 South Pleasant Ave.	**Jessie Adams,** 48
60626	**Chicago**	
	7415 Sheridan Rd.	**Bach,** 193
60628	**Chicago**	
	12147 Harvard Ave.	**Foster Residence** and **Stable,** 49, 50
60637	**Chicago**	
	5757 Woodlawn Ave.	**Robie,** 127
60643	**Chicago**	
	9914 Longwood Dr.	**Evans,** 140
60644	**Chicago**	
	42 North Central Ave.	**Walser,** 91
60653	**Chicago**	
	700 East Oakwood Blvd.	**Abraham Lincoln Center,** 95
60901	**Kankakee**	
	687 South Harrison Ave.	**Hickox,** 56
	701 South Harrison Ave.	**Bradley Residence** and **Stable,** 52, 53
61008	**Belvidere**	
	Harrison at Webster	**Pettit Mortuary Chapel,** 116
61111	**Rockford**	
	Spring Brook Rd.	**Laurent,** 319
61606	**Peoria**	
	1505 West Moss	**Little Residence I** and **Stable,** 70, 71 (**Clarke Additions,** 152)
62522	**Decatur**	
	2 Millikin Pl.	**Irving,** 165
	1 Millikin Pl.	**Mueller,** 167
62703	**Springfield**	
	301-327 East Lawrence Ave.	**Dana Residence** and **Lawrence Memorial Library,** 72, 73

MO Missouri

63122	**Kirkwood**	
	120 North Ballas Rd.	**Kraus,** 340

Missouri (*continued*)

63141	**Saint Louis** 865 South Masonridge Rd.	**Pappas**, 392
64111	**Kansas City** 3600 Bellview Ave.	**Sondern**, 279 (**Adler Addition**, 307)
64112	**Kansas City** 4601 Main St.	**Kansas City Community Christian Church**, 280
64116	**Kansas City** 3640 North Briarcliff Rd.	**Bott**, 404

KS   Kansas

67208	**Wichita** 255 North Roosevelt Blvd. Brolund Dr. at 21st St.	**Allen**, 205 **Juvenile Cultural Study Center**, 418

NE   Nebraska

69001	**McCook** 602 Norris Ave.	**Sutton**, 106

OK   Oklahoma

74003	**Bartlesville** N.E. 6th St. at Dewey Ave.	**Harold Price, Jr.**, 363 **Price Company Tower**, 355
74105	**Tulsa** 3704 South Birmingham Ave.	**Richard Lloyd Jones**, 227

TX   Texas

75219	**Dallas** 3636 Turtle Creek Blvd.	**Dallas Theatre Center**, 395
75220	**Dallas** 9400 Rockbrook Dr.	**Gillin**, 338
77024	**Bunker Hill** 12020 Tall Oaks	**Thaxton**, 384
79606	**Amarillo** Tascosa Rd.	**Sterling Kinney**, 422

WY   Wyoming

82414	**Cody** Greybull Hwy.	**Blair**, 351

ID   Idaho

83314	**Bliss** Old Hagerman Hwy.	**Teater**, 352

UT Utah

84010	**Bountiful** 1151 East North Canyon Rd.	**Stromquist**, 429

AZ Arizona

85013	**Phoenix** 1123 West Palo Verde Dr.	**Carlson.** 326
	6750 North 7th Ave.	**First Christian Church,** A437
85016	**Phoenix** East Sahuaro Dr. at Camino Acequia 5710 North 30th St. 5808 North 30th St. (5800) Orange Rd.	**Arizona Biltmore Hotel** **and Cottages,** 221, 222 **Benjamin Adelman,** 344 **Boomer,** 361 **Pauson,** 250
85018	**Phoenix** 6836 North 36th St. 5212 East Exeter Rd.	**Lykes,** 433 **David Wright** , 322
85258	**Scottsdale** (11000) Shea Rd.	**Pfeiffer,** A434 **Taliesin West,** 241-245
85253	**Paradise Valley** 7211 North Tatum 6442 E. Cheney Rd.	**Harold Price, Sr.,** 378 **Pieper,** 349
85281	**Tempe** Apache Blvd. at Mill Ave.	**Gammage Memorial** **Auditorium,** 432

NM New Mexico

87552	**Pecos**	**Arnold Friedman,** 286

CA California

90027	**Los Angeles** 4800 Hollywood Blvd.	**Barnsdall Hollyhock House,** 208
	4800 Hollywood Blvd.	**Barnsdall Studio Residence A,** 210
	4800 Hollywood Blvd.	**Los Angeles Exhibition Pavilion,** 382
	2607 Glendower Ave.	**Ennis,** 217
90028	**Los Angeles** 1962 Glencoe Way	**Samuel Freeman,** 216
90049	**Brentwood Heights** 449 Skyewiay Rd.	**Sturges,** 272
90069	**Hollywood** 8161 Hollywood Blvd.	**Storer,** 215
90210	**Beverly Hills** 332 North Rodeo Dr.	**Anderton Court Shops,** 356

California (*continued*)

90265 **Malibu**
32436 West Mulholland
Hwy.   **Oboler Gatehouse** and
                              Retreat, 275, 276

91010 **Bradbury**
5 Bradbury Hills Rd.   **Pearce,** 320

91103 **Pasadena**
645 Prospect Crescent   **Mrs. Millard,** 214

93103 **Montecito**
196 Hot Springs Rd.   **Stewart,** 160

93306 **Bakersfield**
4260 Country Club Dr.   **Ablin,** 428

93401 **San Luis Obispo**
1106 Pacific St.   **Kundert Medical Clinic,**
                              396

93635 **Los Banos**
(21200) Center Ave.   **Fawcett,** 385

93921 **Carmel**
Scenic Road at Martin St.   **Walker,** 306

94010 **Hillsborough**
101 Reservoir Rd.   **Bazett,** 259

94025 **Atherton**
83 Wisteria Way   **Mathews,** 331

94108 **San Francisco**
140 Maiden La.   **Morris Gift Shop,** 310

94305 **Stanford**
737 Frenchman's Rd.   **Hanna,** 235

94563 **Orinda**
6 Great Oak Circle   **Buehler,** 309

94704 **Berkeley**
13 Mosswood Rd.   **Feldman,** A436

94903 **San Raphael**
North San Pedro Rd. at   **Marin County Post Office,**
U.S. 101   **Administration Building,**
                              and **Hall of Justice,**
                              415-417

94960 **San Anselmo**
259 Redwood Rd.   **Berger,** 330

95350 **Modesto**
417 Hogue Rd.   **Walton,** 421

96001 **Redding**
2850 Foothill Blvd.   **Congregational Church,**
                              431

OR   Oregon

97002 **Aurora**
South Bank, Willamette   **Gordon,** 419
River

ALPHABETICAL INDEX

Works are indexed by clients and by the boldfaced part of the building titles in the catalog entries. Names of other artists working with Wright and alternate project titles are also included. City listings document all works constructed or located therein. Numbers refer to the catalog entry number. When a name appears in boldface, followed by catalog entry number, without further classification, it refers to a residence.